SOCIAL DEVIANCE

SOCIAL DEVIANCE

DANIEL GLASER
University of Southern California

MARKHAM PUBLISHING COMPANY/Chicago

MARKHAM SERIES IN PROCESS AND CHANGE IN AMERICAN SOCIETY
Robert W. Hodge and David P. Street, Editors

© 1971 Markham Publishing Company
All Rights Reserved
Printed in U.S.A.
Library of Congress Catalog Card Number: 76–163339
Hardcover Standard Book Number: 8410–4201–2
Paperback Standard Book Number: 8410–4204–7

This, like my other writings, is dedicated to my wife, Pearl, not just because she has inspired and facilitated my work, but because her constructive criticism has helped so much in improving it.

CONTENTS

INTRODUCTION

The present volume is one of several in a series on Process and Change in American Society being published by the Markham Publishing Company under our editorship. Each of the volumes in this series is intended to chart the patterns of social change in one of our central institutions and/or in the processes that link these institutions.

As editors, we have encouraged the authors to utilize systematic and quantitative materials wherever they are available. We have also encouraged them to use alternative sources to fill in the appreciable gaps that are left by the quantitative record. Perhaps most important, we have encouraged the authors to present their materials in a provocative way, tying together the scraps of statistical and documentary evidence with a theoretical viewpoint, a central theme, or even a critical perspective informed by articulated ideological principles. Thus, the volumes in this series are intended to be more than summaries of all that is known about social trends and processes of change in the areas on which they focus; they are essays drawing out theoretical and/or policy implications of major substantive conclusions about these areas.

Facts do not speak for themselves, and the volumes in this series are not intended to be written commentaries on statistical abstracts and historical almanacs. Their authors attempt to organize what is known into a more coherent overview from which, hopefully, the reader might both see correctly the interrelations between what is known and surmise the probable character of the missing pieces. Needless to say, when much of the digging around in our past is still to be done, such speculative efforts at organizing known trends can go awry. Therefore, the reader should recognize that, in part, the books draw syntheses that may prove premature when our knowledge is more complete. The reader should also remember that the authors were not charged with filling in the substantive record where it is incomplete. Consequently, some of the conclusions reached are less thoroughly grounded in empirical analysis than would be appropriate in full-scale research monographs. It is hoped, however, that the accounts of change given in these volumes, even when the evidence is piecemeal, will provide guideposts in directions where further excavation is likely to be most productive.

The present volume fulfills the mandate of the series admirably. Professor Glaser provides a lucid discussion of the major forms of deviance in American society, the social processes that give rise to them, and the mechanisms for surveillance and control. His discussion of marginality and the ecology of deviance is especially provocative.

Robert W. Hodge
University of Michigan

David P. Street
State University of New York
at Stony Brook

April, 1971

1
PATTERNS OF DEVIANCE IN THE UNITED STATES

"Deviance," in current American sociology, refers to any behavior or attribute for which an individual is regarded as objectionable in a particular social system. It denotes anything that violates prevailing norms on what makes a person acceptable. Deviance, to a sociologist, does not include acts or attributes that are merely unusual, eccentric, unhealthy, or unwise—such as eating lemon pie with mustard, having one brown eye and one blue, or smoking excessively—as long as they do not make a person objectionable in a given social setting.[1]

A very limited survey found that the types of persons Americans most frequently labelled deviant were homosexuals, drug addicts, and alcoholics. These were followed by somewhat overlapping categories: prostitutes, murderers, criminals, juvenile delinquents, "beatniks," the mentally ill, atheists, Communists, and political extremists (Simmons and Chambers, 1965). Textbooks and collections of readings for sociology courses on deviance cover all the above, as well as suicides, abortionists, nudists, Skid Row derelicts, and even the mentally retarded or physically disabled.[2]

[1] For more elaborate discussions of the definition problem see Cohen, 1966: 1–37; Dinitz, et al., 1969: 3–32; Rubington and Weinberg, 1968: 1–12; Rushing, 1969: 1–3.
[2] See the tables of contents of Clinard, 1968; Cohen, 1966; Dinitz, et al., 1969; Lefton, et al., 1968; Rubington and Weinberg, 1968; Rushing, 1969.

Obviously, deviance connotes a broad, mixed, vaguely defined, and fluctuating assortment of conduct and characteristics. About all they have in common is the reaction they arouse.[3] At some time, in some social situations, each has been a widespread basis for people's viewing other people as objectionable. Such reactions to deviance have played a prominent part in American history.

LIFE IN AMERICA AS A CONSEQUENCE OF DEVIANCE

Persons who conform to the norms in a country and are successful there—by prevailing standards—are least likely to leave that country voluntarily. Those who fail more often seek "greener pastures" elsewhere, and those who are defined by the dominant groups as deviant are made uncomfortable or even expelled. America, long the frontier for Europe, was the haven to which deviants and failures flocked or were deported.

The most familiar example of this behavior is the flight of religious deviants from Europe to become American colonists. Puritans persecuted in England sought refuge in Holland, but were still a deviant minority there. They came to America to found their own community, which became the Massachusetts Bay Colony. William Penn, jailed for promoting Quaker beliefs in England, established the Commonwealth of Pennsylvania for his coreligionists. After Catholics lost dominance in Britain, George Calvert (Lord Baltimore) gave some a haven in Maryland. Refuge could be obtained by these religious groups only because some of them had resources. Their leaders were landed gentry with means and influence in Britain, with which they bargained for large land grants in the colonies and procured transportation and capital necessary to establish a viable economy in the wilderness. Not all emigrants were that fortunate. Indeed, not all of them came to America voluntarily.

At the beginning of the eighteenth century Britons convicted of felonies were given a choice between death and transportation

---

[3] ". . . deviance is not a quality of the act the person commits, but . . . a consequence of the application by others of rules and sanctions to an 'offender.'" (Becker, 1963: 9).

to the American colonies. By 1718 transportation was the standard penalty in Britain for felonious theft. It has been estimated that as many as a thousand criminals were sentenced every year to exile in what was later to become the United States. At first the Crown paid for this transportation, but soon American colonists were eager to pay these fees in exchange for use of convicts as indentured servants. British sea captains then found it profitable to carry convicts across the ocean at no cost to their government (Rusche and Kirchheimer, 1939: 58–62, 114–123).

The convicts generally were brought to Virginia, Maryland, Georgia, or the Carolinas, and were freed after three years of service. Some escaped earlier and helped settle the hinterland. American demand for British convicts declined with the rise of the African slave trade, for slaves were owned more completely and permanently than indentured servants were. After the American Revolution, Britain sent her convicts to other colonies, notably Australia. Francis Bacon condemned this practice, calling it "a shameful and unblessed thing to take the scum of people, and wicked and condemned men, to be the people with whom you plant. . . ." The convicts, however, generally became respected citizens wherever they had opportunities to establish new lives for themselves (Rusche and Kirchheimer, 1939: 58–62, 114–123; Jernegan, 1929: 96, 102, 316).

Deviants in a given community are by definition conformists in any other community where they have power to enforce their standards on others. Thus the definition of deviance is a relative matter, a function of who has power to determine what is acceptable. Great fluctuations have occurred in the extent to which certain types of behavior have been considered objectionable, while other types have been quite continuously and universally regarded as deviant. Therefore, the relativity of deviance is not uniform and invariant.

MAJOR VARIATIONS IN THE DEFINITIONS AND DIMENSIONS OF DEVIANCE

Criminals may be thought of by many as, by definition, deviant. This view overlooks areas of nonoverlap between crime and deviance, and more important, the diversity of both. While deviance includes all acts for which people are classified as violating normative standards in a social system, crime refers only to those acts for which a court may lawfully impose punishment. Discrepancies exist between these two classifications of behavior and these discrepancies vary from time to time and from one legal jurisdiction to another. Thus Illinois in 1961 was the first state to enact a law that made homosexual acts between consenting adults in private no longer a crime. Nevertheless, such acts did not suddenly become nondeviant in Illinois in 1961 and remain deviant elsewhere. The designation of behavior as deviant is a matter of predominant public consensus, and this changes only gradually; the designation of an act as punishable by the state, and hence a crime, is a legislative event or judicial interpretation at a particular time and place that is only roughly correlated with trends in the public's conception of deviance.

Chronic alcoholism is regarded as deviant, but it is not criminal in itself, and being intoxicated is only criminal under certain circumstances, primarily in public places or while driving an automobile. Most types of deviance have at times been legally punished and at times not been punished; some deviance is almost always crime and some is never crime. As this implies, both deviance and crime are diverse.

Deviance can be classified into at least seven broad categories of behavior or condition that differ markedly in the consistency with which they have been regarded as deviant, and in their estimated prevalence in the United States. Independently of these variations, they also differ in whether or not they are criminal. In addition, as shown in later chapters, they are heterogeneous in causes and consequences. These categories are predation, deviant consumption, deviant selling, deviant performance, deviant belief, suicide, and deviant attributes.

Predation

These are acts in which someone definitely and intentionally takes or damages the person or property of another. These acts clearly involve two distinct roles: predator and victim. They are what we most commonly connote by "crime."

The two major types of predation are offenses against property—taking a victim's money or goods—or, offenses against persons—injuring a victim. Offenses against property include theft, burglary, forgery, and fraud, while those against persons include assault, rape, kidnapping, and homicide. Robbery, a mixture of the two, consists of taking property from someone by force or threat of force.

Acts of predation are almost universally regarded as deviance when committed against members of one's own group, although they are tolerated against enemy nationals in wartime. The definition of predation as objectionable also varies somewhat within most social systems according to the relationship of the predator to the victim and the nature of the predation. For example, much fraud against the government by tax evasion, or against an indefinite public by misrepresentation in selling, is not usually regarded as deviant in the United States, even when punishable as crime. Conversely, predation usually is deviant but not criminal if committed by persons below a legally determined age, or by persons legally classified as noncriminal because of their mental ailments or defects. Despite these exceptions and variations, public definition of much in-group predation as deviance, and much as also criminal, is relatively constant and universal.

The relationship between state action against in-group predation and economic development was ingeniously demonstrated by Freeman and Winch (1957). Through ordinal scaling of forty-eight societies of diverse complexity, they showed dramatically that where government institutions have not developed to punish predators, the society also rarely has replaced barter by a money system. Without a money system, commerce and industry have little prospect of growth to the levels needed for a modern economy.

Police and courts, to combat the disorder that comes both from predation and from private vengeance-seeking, permit the development of large-scale organizations for industrial production, trade, and finance. Such organizations, however, plus technological innovations, create new kinds of predation (for example, check forgery, stock swindles, or auto theft). Economic systems involving the complex monetary transactions and obligations that are conducted by banks and stock markets survive only if victimization is kept to a minimum. Especially since the Renaissance and the Commercial Revolution, there has been a steady increase in the range of predation considered so threatening to society that the state intervenes, replacing private by public revenge through calling it "crime" (Hall, 1952). The variety of predatory behavior called criminal has, with negligible exception, changed in only one direction—cumulatively. This relationship of the diversity of predation regarded as criminal to technology and to the complexity and scale of organizations is a relationship that occurs in both capitalist and socialist economies.

Because it is assumed that victims of predation report their victimization to law enforcement authorities, the frequency of predation is usually measured by counting predatory crimes known to the police. National totals are difficult to acquire with precision, however, because there are approximately 40,000 separate police forces in the United States, each autonomous in recordkeeping, and because legal labels and definitions for predatory crimes vary somewhat among the fifty states, the District of Columbia, and various other federal jurisdictions. Nevertheless, since 1930 the Federal Bureau of Investigation has attempted to standardize and collate data on such offenses in its *Uniform Crime Reports,* and has made impressive progress in this difficult task.

To minimize confusion from diverse designations, FBI statistics on crimes known to the police are limited to seven so-called Index offenses: murder, rape, aggravated assault, burglary, theft (or "larceny") of $50 or more, and auto theft. This selection is justified because "the crimes used in the Crime Index are those considered to be most consistently reported to police. . . ." (Federal Bureau of Investigation, 1970: 9).

According to the FBI, these seven "Index" predations increased in rate each year from about 1,000 per 100,000 population during 1960 to almost 2,500 in 1969. This increase was greatest in robbery and theft and smallest in murder. To evaluate this trend, however, one must first assess the validity of these statistics.

In 1965–66 the President's Commission on Law Enforcement and Administration of Justice had researchers ask a national sample of households if their occupants were in the preceding year victims of any of the seven Index offenses. These offenses were reported more than twice as often as the FBI's rates would lead one to expect. The discrepancies between victim survey research data and rates reported to police were negligible for murder and auto theft, but they indicated that police data on crime omit three-fourths of rapes, two-thirds of burglaries, half the aggravated assaults, half the thefts of $50 or more and a third of robberies (President's Commission, 1967: 20ff.). For a variety of reasons, people do not report all predations to the police, and sometimes the police fail to tabulate those in which the victim does notify them. These discrepancies between victim survey data and FBI statistics raise the interesting question of whether apparent increases in crime rates during the 1960s were not mostly increases in the proportion of predations reported to the police and recorded by them.

The first sign of an improved police system is often what is most embarrassing to police administrators—a sharp increase in crime rates. Thus Kansas City between 1959 and 1961 tripled its rate of Index offenses; Buffalo between 1961 and 1963 doubled its rates; Chicago in 1959 and 1960 had a 72 percent increase (President's Commission, 1967: 25). These upsurges reflect more complete recording by the police, and perhaps more complete reporting of crimes to the police as the public gains confidence in law enforcement. The FBI, by excluding data from cities with such dramatic jumps in crime rate, concludes from the remaining communities that the increase of Index offense crime rates in the United States during the 1960s was 120 percent, rather than the 150 percent suggested by the rise from about 1,000 to 2,500 per 100,000 population. But they cannot know how much of the 120 percent reflects only more gradual increases in other communities, in percent of victims reporting predation to the police, and in the completeness of recording by the police. Improved recording should have resulted from the rapid growth in staff and advances in training and use of electronic data processing that characterized most U.S. police forces in the 1960s and 1970s.

The best way to measure such trends in completeness of police statistics, and simultaneously to assess public attitudes towards the police, is to repeat routinely the kinds of victim survey research initiated by the President's Commission (Glaser, 1969). Despite hundreds of millions of dollars expended annually for "law enforcement assistance" by the federal government, regular victim survey research as a law enforcement accounting resource was still in only an exploratory stage in 1971, so trends in completeness of reporting to police could still not be measured.

While automobile theft rates in relation to population increased 168 percent in the 1960s according to the FBI, increase in such theft in relation to the number of automobiles in the country was not as great. In 1950 there were 36 million cars in the United States; by 1960 there were 57 million; and by 1969—the latest year for which we could obtain data—there were 78 million. The FBI reported 318,520 auto thefts in the United States in 1960, or 560 per 100,000 cars, while in 1969 it reported 871,900 or 1,118 per 100,000 cars. In this ten year period the rate of auto theft per 100,000 people increased 168 percent, but the rate per 100,000 automobiles increased 100 percent. The percentage of families in the United States owning two or more automobiles increased from 15 percent in 1960 to 27 percent in 1969; greater affluence created more automobiles to steal (FBI, 1970; Bureau of the Census, 1970).

Rising affluence in the postwar years was evident not just with automobiles, but also in the increase of portable appliances (television sets, tape recorders, and the like) and in the inflationary trend in all prices. These account for some of the rise in reported burglary and theft of items worth $50 or more, rather than an increase in the proportion of total propety that was stolen. The 1960s also saw a tremendous increase of theft insurance on personal property. This increase was due to its heavy sales promotion in this period as part of a single homeowner's policy covering theft as well as the more customary—and often mandatory—fire, storm, and public liability. In some cities, notably New York, "renter's policies" also were widely sold, to cover personal goods only. Such insurance created a new motivation to report crimes to the police— to collect compensation from insurance companies—for they required that police be notified. Thus we cannot know how much of the increase in property predation known to the police reflects trends in crime and how much reflects these other developments.

Murder—or to be technically more accurate, nonnegligent homicide—probably is the most accurately counted type of predation despite some occasional ambiguity in distinguishing it from death by accident or suicide. It is reported in both police and public health statistics, the latter based on physicians' reports on the causes of death. Rates from these two sources have differed only slightly in recent years. A striking feature of murder rates was their decline from a peak of 9.6 per 100,000 in 1933 to a low of 4.5 in 1955–58 by U.S. Public Health Service data, and from 7.1 in 1933 to 4.5 in 1962–63 by FBI data. Both statistical series rose slowly thereafter, the FBI rate reaching a peak of 7.2 for 1969. (There is a lag of eight months in publication of annual data by the FBI, and of about two years in the *Vital Statistics* of the U.S. Public Health Service.)

One cause of rising predation rates in the 1960s and 1970s was an increase in the population at the age range when these rates are highest. As indicated in Chapter Three, the median ages of arrest for burglary, theft, and auto theft are between 17 and 18; for robbery, aggravated assault, and murder they are 20, 27, and 28, respectively. The post-World War II baby boom created, fifteen to thirty years later, a burgeoning population with ages of peak predation rate.

Assault and rape, which are never completely reported to the police, are also less than fully reported to survey researchers, since people are especially embarrassed to report victimization by these offenses. Because of ambiguity in the definitions of rape and of aggravated assault, and the frequent withdrawal of complaints after tempers have cooled, these are the two types of Index offense police most often fail to record when they are reported, or record as "unfounded" and do not tabulate. Therefore, it is for these predations that FBI rates probably are most markedly affected by trends in proportion of offenses reported and recorded, independently of trends in actual occurrence of the offenses.

Acts initiated as assault, robbery, and rape often culminate as nonnegligent homicide when a lethal weapon is at hand. The 1960s saw a marked increase in the sale of handguns to the general population and a consequent rise, from about half to nearly two-thirds, in the proportion of murders in which death was inflicted by handguns. The greater prevalence of guns and the higher concentration of population in assaultive age ranges suffice to account for most of the increase from less than five to a peak of over seven homicides per 100,000 persons per year during the 1960s.

Statistics on predation for the first part of the twentieth century and for earlier periods are not available on a national basis, but have been collected in a fairly uniform and complete manner by a few of our older cities. They are based on arrests, however, rather than on crimes known to the police, and thus reflect in part any changes in the percentage of crimes known to the police that they "clear" by arrest. Data for Boston murders show a predominantly downward trend, despite periods of fluctuation, from more than 7 per 100,000 persons per year in the middle of the nineteenth century to less than two per 100,000 per year a hundred years later. Assaults varied in close correlation with murder rates in Boston as they do in most other jurisdictions in all periods. In about a century from 1849 to 1951, however, reported rapes rose from an annual rate of less than two to more than a dozen per 100,000 population. Robberies fluctuated greatly with economic conditions; their peak of over 45 per 100,000 per year came in the Great Depression of the 1930s. Burglaries also had their highest rates of the 1849–1951 period in the late 1930s, but larcenies declined fairly steadily from a peak rate in the 1850s. During this period, however, there appears to have been a marked decline in the proportion of minor property crimes that the police solved by arrest; this probably accounts for the downward trends in larceny arrest rates during this century (Ferdinand, 1967). Fairly similar trends in arrest rate are tabulated in detail for Buffalo in the century 1854–1956, and are reported also for several other cities (Powell, 1966).

Deviant consumption

This behavior consists of using certain goods or services deemed objectionable by those dominating a social system. At various times and places this deviance has included the use of substances such as alcohol, marijuana, opiates, and inhalant glue, or of services such as prostitution, abortion, homosexual response, and gambling. These acts have no clear victim; the people who consider this consumption objectionable may regard the deviant himself as the victim and refer to the activity as a "vice" or an abuse of oneself, but the deviant often—perhaps usually—does not share this view. The designation of types of consumption as deviant has varied greatly in most societies, but especially in twentieth-century United States.

During periods of change in the definition of any form of consumption as deviance, there is much controversy over the somewhat separate issues of (1) whether it is objectionable and (2) whether it should be punishable as violation of criminal law. Because of technical problems of constitutionality or enforceability, illegal consumption is sometimes not a crime even when predominantly viewed as deviant. For example, *use* of narcotics, as distinguished from possession or sale, is not a crime in the United States, and as mentioned earlier, private voluntary homosexuality between adults is not a crime in Illinois. Sometimes, for various reasons, consumption of a service is criminal in certain settings and not in others. For example, in most of the United States off-track betting is illegal but on-track betting is not, and neither is widely viewed as deviant when not pursued to excess. Finally, because of inertia in law-changing, or of the disproportionate influence of well-organized or high-status minorities engaged in law making, some types of consumption may be criminal even when they are predominantly not viewed as deviant. An example was consumption of alcohol in many areas during the period immediately preceding repeal of prohibition laws.

Because of all these conditions, designation of certain types of consumption as criminal has become the basis for major political controversies in the United States (see Chapter Six). There is conflict over whether certain types of consumption—marijuana, alcohol and abortion for instance—should be crimes, and this conflict is often cited by those who emphasize the relativity of deviance and of crime. The popular conception of particular types of consumption as deviance, and their legal designation as crimes, have fluctuated much more than have views and laws defining other behavior as deviant or criminal. Therefore, while study of deviant consumption leads some to conclude that what is called deviance or crime reflects only which group is strongest in a social conflict, such an image does not easily fit those predatory acts that have defined victims. These acts have had a much less variant designation as both deviant and criminal. There is, in fact, predominant and continuous agreement on the classification of many types of in-group predation as crime, even by those who commit them.

Because deviant consumption is pursued voluntarily, the deviant does not usually consider himself a victim and report his activity to the police. Therefore, rates of such deviance—for example, homosexuality, use of narcotics, or being served by prostitutes—cannot be determined from number of cases known to the police. Police information varies as much with the extent of their investment in entrapment, surveillance, or use of informants as with actual occurrence of these forms of deviance in the community.

It follows that the primary method for estimating prevalence of deviant consumption is survey research. A Gallup Poll in 1969 reported that 4 percent of Americans 21 years of age or over admitted having used marijuana. For those 21 through 29 years old, the figure was 12 percent. In a December 1970 poll limited to college students the rate was 42 percent. The percentages were even higher for college students in their senior or graduate years and for those in the social sciences. In a U.S. Army survey about a third of enlisted men in Vietnam admitted marijuana use. Because deviant activity is widely condemned, and may even be severely punishable as crime, it is likely that admissions to survey researchers are incomplete. The figures probably err in the direction of underestimating actual prevalence rates.

A variety of less obtrusive indices of deviant consumption are also available. For example, one may estimate trends in off-track gambling on horse races from sales of the *Daily Racing Form* and of turf editions of daily newspapers in northern cities during the winter, when local tracks are not in use. One can estimate dimensions of prostitution by frequency with which one is solicited in given areas. The prevalence of homosexuality is often inferred from visibility of its least seclusive proponents in some neighborhoods.

All of the indices illustrated above reflect both variations in the occurrence of these types of deviant consumption and variations in tolerance for their visibility or for their commercial exploitation. From such imperfect evidence it is widely believed that the range of consumption that is acceptable—hence nondeviant—in the United States has grown markedly in recent decades. Essentially, the prevalence of some types of deviant consumption has increased to the point where these types no longer are considered deviant in large segments of American communities; this trend is likely to continue for other types of nonvictimizing deviance. Details of such trends and their causes are analyzed in Chapter Six.

Deviant selling

A counterpart of deviant consumption is the act of supplying consumers with goods or services others regard as objectionable. This is viewed as distinctly deviant when done for money. Selling is considered separately from consumption here, because often only the selling of the goods or services—not their utilization—is designated as deviance, or only selling is classified as crime. Thus the prostitute, and especially the panderer or pimp, are generally considered more deviant or criminal than the prostitute's patron; the patron is often not judged objectionable at all while the pimp is stigmatized. In addition, so-called organized crime for the sale of deviant services may have very different consequences for society, as a strain on political and judicial institutions, than does the consumption of the services it provides. Not only is it true that the deviant seller and the consumer differ greatly in their orientations to each other; the seller also differs radically from the consumer in his relationships with a large illegal organization and with law-enforcement and judicial officials.

The nature of deviant selling and its consequences are functions of the supply of goods and services in relationship to the demand. Opiate addiction is distinctive for the extreme physiological imbalance created by the sudden cessation of use. An addict's demand for more drugs is therefore highly inelastic; he will pay almost any price necessary to procure opiates. Consequently, those who engage in this type of deviant consumption frequently procure funds for their purchases by committing property predation or by various types of deviant selling. Such willingness to use any means to satisfy their craving also is common among chronic alcoholics, but the cost of their addiction rarely is as great as that of dependence on opiates, and their drink can be purchased from nondeviant sellers—liquor stores instead of "moonshiners."

Deviant selling in which demand is relatively elastic, such as prostitution and organized off-track gambling services, frequently requires active solicitation of sales. This entails public visibility, and if sales are illegal, the police must be corrupted to permit visibility. Known "bookie joints" and numbers operations, therefore, are essentially licensed by the police in that they can only operate as extensively and openly as they do with police knowledge and permission. Usually, corruption of police is part of a larger penetration by illegal selling organizations into presumably legitimate organizations. It has been estimated that 15 percent of political contributions in the United States come from organized crime—illegal selling groups who are also widely involved in legitimate business and financial activity (Cressey, 1969: 253).

The decline in some types of deviant selling during the 1960s and 1970s were claimed by the U.S. Department of Justice to be the result of their greatly expanded prosecutions of organized crime. It is probable, however, that an even more influential source of the decline in selling is reduction of the market. Prostitution has probably declined, for example, because premarital sexual activity has become more prevalent and acceptable, hence nondeviant. Gambling has also become more widely legalized and accepted as nondeviant. Use of some types of drugs, notably marijuana, has become so widespread that the selling involved in its distribution must have grown tremendously in recent years. Though still illegal, it is apparently less widely regarded as deviant than formerly.

Deviant performance

This category encompasses a large range of behavior that, while not aimed at injuring anyone, nevertheless offends some audiences who complain effectively. Therefore, while such behavior is regarded as deviant when manifested in public places, it usually is not considered objectionable if done in private. Nudity and drunkenness are generally viewed as deviant and possibly criminal only if they occur in public places. No objection is voiced even if they are admitted to have occurred in private. Most arrests in the United States are for "disorderly conduct" and "public drunkenness." A majority of these, as well as arrests for "vagrancy" and "loitering," are for public display of symptoms of chronic alcoholism; others are for symptoms of schizophrenia, or for behavior creating suspicion of illegal drug trafficking, when the latter cannot be proven. To be considered "crazy"—as overtly expressing mental illness—is to be regarded as deviant.

The distinction between types of deviant performance for which punishment as crime is lawful and types for which medical treatment is prescribed is in practice often extremely blurred. This lack of clarity apparently reflects two processes of redefinition now in progress. First, some forms of consumption are now regarded as deviant only if they are manifested to particular types of audiences: they are only deviant as *performances*. This phenomenon is reflected in the greater acceptance of homosexuality and other deviant forms of sexual expression in the theater and at nightclubs but not in more public places. It is evident in objections to drinking and gambling where children are present. This kind of differentiation may also be occurring with marijuana use.

Second, there is a shift occurring in official labelling and restriction of deviant activity. Much that was once regarded as crime is now defined as mental illness, and some behavior once regarded as mental illness is now accepted as nondeviant. Beginning in the late 1960s, for example, arrests for drunkenness declined somewhat each year largely through the provision of "detoxification" facilities in many large cities. Police deliver drunken persons to these stations for medical and social work services. The population of state mental hospitals also declined, partly because of laws making it more difficult to commit a person involuntarily and partly because of greater tolerance in the community for behavior that once caused persons to be rejected as mentally deviant.

Deviant belief

Alleged adherence to particular ideas, usually on religion or politics, has been one of the most widespread yet variable bases for defining people as deviant. This is especially true of religion. Almost every religious group that has ever predominated in an area has earlier struggled for existence as a deviant and persecuted sect. The deaths of hundreds of thousands in Catholic-Protestant conflicts in seventeenth century Europe, as well as in Hindu-Moslem rioting in mid-twentieth century India, are prominent examples of the dimensions of reaction to what is regarded as religious deviance. Indeed, religious intolerance of extreme intensity and great variety has occurred on every continent, in all centuries. Extensive tolerance of atypical religions is a relatively recent phenomenon historically, and such tolerance is still far from universal.

Those who fled to America to escape objection to their religious views eventually gained power to determine what faiths would be tolerated in their new communities. Groups differed in their reactions to beliefs other than their own. The Puritans, although themselves oppressed in Britain, became notorious in Massachusetts for persecution of Baptists, Quakers, Antinomians, and others (Erikson, 1966). In contrast the Quakers, though harassed almost everywhere except in Pennsylvania, welcomed and even actively recruited non-Quakers; tolerance was a basic tenet of their creed (Dunn, 1967; Jernegan, 1929: 208–212, 233–234).

A distinctive feature of the entire United States at its origin was the toleration of religious diversity expressed in the First Amendment to the Constitution. Yet local practice did not always conform to this national precept. The Mormons were the most prominent of numerous groups driven out of American communities because of their faith. While persecution of persons because of their religious views has not disappeared from all corners of the United States, those persecuted for such views today comprise only a minute percentage of all persons regarded as deviant in this country.

The U.S. Constitution has also been a model for the legal protection of diversity in political belief. However, a quasi-religious fervor has often characterized both support for and reaction against certain political ideas and affiliations. Abolitionists were stoned as deviants in Boston before the Civil War, alleged anarchists were persecuted in America during the World War I era, and in post-World War II years there has been much reaction in the United States against Communists and their alleged sympathizers. Nevertheless, neither deviant religion nor deviant political belief per se is criminal in the United States. The exception is advocacy of overthrow of the government by force, in a manner that a court finds is "a clear and present danger."

It is difficult to assess trends in political deviance because so much that is regarded as deviant in one period becomes acceptable in a later period. On the whole, the long-term drift has been in the opposite direction from what is considered conservative at any given time. Therefore, much that is regarded as "radical" in one era becomes "liberal" subsequently and ultimately "middle of the road" or even "conservative." These shifts occurred in the United States between the 1920s and the 1970s, in varying degrees, for support of government-financed old age pensions, unemployment insurance, labor's right to collective bargaining, federal aid to the educationally deprived in communities with low tax resources, and government payment for medical services for the general population.

As the rate of technological change and consequent social and economic maladjustment accelerates, the rate at which new solutions are proposed and become political issues also increases. To be regarded as clearly deviant the advocate of political change has to be perceived as challenging basic norms or values of the society, not simply non-normative beliefs or practices. It is characteristic of periods of collective emotion over any issue that people resolve tension by explaining events through what Smelser calls a "generalized belief"—a more abstract norm or value seen as encompassing the specific matter in controversy. Thus an issue of minority group employment in the construction trades is reformulated. Members of the minority consider it as a right to equality. Those with access to such jobs view their position as a right to a trade they worked hard to learn and to pass on to their sons. Similarly, an issue of union contracts for farm workers is expressed by the workers as a right to fair treatment and by the employers as a right of freedom to hire whom they prefer. When the complex analysis needed for a rational alleviation of specific sources of tension is not readily possible, the ambiguity and frustration that the tension creates are reduced by what Smelser calls the "short-circuiting" of complex thought through appeal to a generalized belief (Smelser, 1963).

Polarization of beliefs in a society is indicated by the dimensions of its extremist or its "value oriented" social movements (Smelser, 1963). In the United States this phenomenon reached a peak in the Civil War, but it is well measured at other times in our history by the votes achieved by extremist political parties. Thus far these have never had more than a brief and local hegemony, as the issues underlying their support eventually are resolved either by a change of events (such as the end of an economic recession) or by a change in prevalent beliefs (for example, acceptance of desegregation), accompanied by co-optation of their followers by major political parties.

The most distinctive feature of a system of democratic representative government with a relatively high degree of freedom for expressing deviant beliefs is its ability to change peacefully. It seems true, as Lipset and others have asserted, that revolution is impossible in the United States or in other countries with well-established institutions of representative government (Lipset, 1960, 1963). Because regular and relatively free elections occur with acceptance of the rule that the election winners take office only for their lawful terms, all parties try to win the next election by appealing to all large segments of voters.

In the second half of the twentieth century in the United States, issues of equality of opportunity for racial groups in voting, jobs, housing, and other matters repeatedly polarized large minorities of the population, but the polarization repeatedly ebbed as dominant parties made some concessions on demands gaining wide support. This diminished support for the most politically deviant organizations. Thus far, before revolutionary movements of any sort have been able to gain anything remotely near the prospect of overthrowing the government of the United States, their followers have been lured away by major parties making concessions and by a subsequent reduction in the level of general discontent. In this way some demands unique to the Communist and Socialist party platforms in the 1920s—such as the call for recognition of a right to collective bargaining by unions, and for insurance against unemployment—became laws passed by the majority parties in the 1930s, without adoption of the other items in the extremist party platforms that never gained large-scale public support.

It is also a noteworthy observation, not adequately analyzed and explained in social science literature, that independent countries in which a majority of the adult population participate in regular elections with a free choice between alternative candidates, have never engaged in wars with each other—except civil wars and wars of colonies against the countries that rule over them. The stipulation of a majority of the adult population excludes Great Britain before the extension of franchise in its Great Reform Act of 1832, and it excludes France in those periods of the nineteenth century when it lacked elected representative governments (Babst, 1964). The implication appears to be that world peace will be secure when representative elections are firmly institutionalized in all countries, or in a world government.

Suicide

In all societies, killing oneself is viewed as either a deviant or a conforming act, depending upon the circumstances in which it is done. To kill oneself so that others may live, as in falling on a grenade to save one's fellow soldiers, is the highest type of normative conformity, but to kill oneself to avoid the pains and struggles of living is viewed as deviant. In many societies suicide as a conforming act has been ritualized under certain conditions, as in the Trobriands after incest is exposed, in pre-war Japan as *hara-kiri* following dishonor, and in former years in India, as the *suttee* custom of a widow throwing herself upon her husband's flaming funeral pyre. In some jurisdictions it is a crime to attempt suicide, but the law is enforceable only if the attempt is unsuccessful. The would-be suicide, however, is usually treated as mentally ill.

Estimates of the number of people in the United States who at some time in their life have attempted suicide range from two million to five million, and it is believed that about one-tenth these numbers make an attempt each year. The number who succeed in killing themselves has ranged from 21,000 to 22,000 in recent years, a rate of about 11 per 100,000 population. This is slightly lower than the peak suicide rate of 12.5 in 1932 during the Great Depression and slightly above its low point of 9.8 in 1957 (Mintz, 1970; Bureau of the Census, 1970).

It is quite probable that official suicide rates are always much lower than actual rates. This is because some people are able to make their deliberate self-destruction appear to be an accident or because family members and physicians will report a death as due to accidental or natural causes to avoid the stigma of suicide (Wilkins, 1970). Such cases need not invalidate our generalizations on trends in suicide or on the relative rank in suicide rate of various groups within the total population, where it seems reasonable to assume that the percentage error in the rate is approximately the same proportion in all periods and groups compared.

The suicide rate in the United States has generally been about 60 percent of rates in Sweden, Denmark, and West Germany, which are approximately 19 per 100,000 per year. During various years of the 1960s rates of 34 and 24 per 100,000, respectively, were reported for Hungary and Czechoslovakia and a rate of over 40 was reported for West Berlin, while Japan and France had rates of 14 or 15. Italy, however, had only five or six suicides per 100,000 persons per year, and Ireland's rate was half of this (United Nations, 1970).

National variations may be explained by generally higher rates for Protestants than for Catholics, regardless of country, but this does not account for the high French and German figures, or for relatively low rates in Norway.

Suicide rates in almost all countries are two or three times as high for men as for women and are higher for urban than for rural populations. They increase with age, especially for men, reaching a level after age 45 about twice that in the early twenties. Divorced persons, especially males, have much higher suicide rates than married persons, with rates for single and widowed persons intermediate. High suicide rates are found among persons of professional and managerial occupations, on the one hand, and unskilled, on the other, with occupations between these statuses (semiskilled, skilled, and white collar workers, for example) lower in suicide rates. Rates for whites in the United States have been about three times those for U.S. nonwhites.

Compared to most other rates of deviance in the United States, the suicide rate appears to have been fairly constant in recent years. What seems to be occurring, however, is a movement toward convergence in rates for the two sexes, for the various racial groups, and for urban and rural populations; this movement, however, is still far from complete. Such a convergence presumably reflects a reduction in the differences between these groups in occupational pursuits, and in consequent insecurity and sense of relative deprivation. Evidence and inference on the causes of suicide will be presented in Chapter Four.

Deviant attributes

Being a midget or an amputee, being spastic or otherwise poorly coordinated muscularly (usually a consequence of neural ailments or muscle atrophy), being very atypical in facial features (either by heredity or due to a severe accident), being blind or deaf and dumb, or being mentally defective may result in a person's being treated as objectionable in many communities, organizations, or other social systems. Indeed, being of a minority racial or national descent has also been regarded as objectionable in many social settings, and may thus also be classified as deviance. All of these are somewhat marginal to much use of the concept "deviance," since these are conditions rather than acts, and thus cannot be called "deviant behavior." In terms of the reaction they arouse, however, they certainly have much similarity to other forms of deviance (on the blind, for example, see Scott, 1969).

Possession of these deviant attributes has never been called crime in the United States to any appreciable or sustained extent, but there has been much enforcement of criminal laws whereby persons actually were punished primarily for these deviant attributes rather than for the criminal acts with which they were charged. Most deviants have a higher-than-average probability of suffering injustice when criminally prosecuted on charges unrelated to their deviance, because many people making judicial decisions may allow their repugnance towards the accused's deviance to impair the objectivity with which they weigh the charges against him.

REFERENCES

Babst, Dean V.
  1964   "Elective governments—a force for peace," Wisconsin
          Sociologist 3 (January): 9–14.
Becker, Howard S.
  1963   Outsiders. New York: Free Press.
Bureau of the Census, U.S. Department of Commerce
  1970   Statistical Abstract of the United States: 1969. Wash-
          ington: U.S. Government Printing Office.
Clinard, Marshall B.
  1968   Sociology of Deviant Behavior, 3rd ed. New York: Holt,
          Rinehart and Winston.
Cohen, Albert K.
  1966   Deviance and Control. Englewood Cliffs, N.J.: Prentice-
          Hall.
Cressey, Donald R.
  1969   Theft of the Nation. New York: Harper and Row.
Dinitz, Simon, Russell R. Dynes and Alfred C. Clarke
  1969   Deviance. New York: Oxford University Press.
Dunn, Mary M.
  1967   William Penn. Princeton, N.J.: Princeton University
          Press.
Erikson, Kai T.
  1966   Wayward Puritans. New York: Wiley.
Federal Bureau of Investigation, U.S. Department of Justice
  1970   Uniform Crime Reports—1969. Washington: U.S. Gov-
          ernment Printing Office.
Ferdinand, Theodore N.
  1967   "The criminal patterns of Boston since 1849." Ameri-
          can Journal of Sociology 73 (July): 84–99.
Freeman, Linton C., and Robert F. Winch
  1957   "Societal complexity: an empirical test of a typology
          of societies." American Journal of Sociology 62
          (March): 461–466.
Glaser, Daniel
  1969   "Victim survey research: theoretical implications." In

Anthony L. Guenther (ed.), Criminal Behavior and Social Systems. Chicago: Rand McNally.

Hall, Jerome
1952   Theft, Law and Society, 2d ed. Indianapolis: Bobbs-Merrill.

Jernegan, Marcus W.
1929   The American Colonies, 1492–1650. New York: Longmans Green.

Lefton, Mark, James K. Skipper, Jr., and Charles H. McCaghy
1968   Approaches to Deviance. New York: Appleton-Century-Crofts.

Lipset, Seymour Martin
1960   Political Man. Garden City, N.Y.: Doubleday.
1963   The First New Nation. New York: Basic Books.

Mintz, Ronald S.
1970   "Prevalence of persons in the city of Los Angeles who have attempted suicide: a pilot study," Bulletin of Suicidology 7 (Fall): 9–16.

Powell, Elwin H.
1966   "Crime as a function of anomie," Journal of Criminal Law, Criminology and Police Science 57 (June): 161–171.

President's Commission on Law Enforcement and the Administration of Justice
1967   The Challenge of Crime in a Free Society. Washington: U.S. Government Printing Office.

Rubington, Earl, and Martin S. Weinberg
1968   Deviance: the Interactionist Perspective. New York: Macmillan.

Rusche, Georg, and Otto Kirchheimer
1939   Punishment and Social Structure. New York: Columbia University Press.

Rushing, William A.
1969   Deviant Behavior and Social Process. Chicago: Rand McNally.

Scott, Robert A.
1969   The Making of Blind Men: A Study of Adult Socialization. New York: Russell Sage Foundation.

Simmons, Jerry L., and Hazel Chambers
   1965   "Public stereotypes of deviants." Social Problems 15 (Fall): 223–232.
Smelser, Neil J.
   1963   Theory of Collective Behavior. New York: Free Press.
United Nations
   1970   Demographic Yearbook: 1969. New York: United Nations.
Wilkins, James L.
   1970   "Producing suicides." American Behavioral Scientist 14 (November/December): 185–201.

2
FRONTIERS AND THE ECOLOGY OF DEVIANCE

As suggested earlier in discussing settlement of the American colonies, people who are treated as objectionable tend to move to locations where there is more tolerance of diversity. These areas, therefore, acquire high concentrations of persons regarded elsewhere as deviant. The nearest places of security for deviance are, of course, just beyond the borders of regions where deviance is suppressed. Thus America was a collecting ground for the deviants of Europe, and within America, the western frontier was long the area to which deviants moved from the eastern settlements.

In the American West, pioneering attracted adventurers, but many of them were more driven than drawn to the western adventureland. In frontier towns and cities the mobile population, the huge distances between communities, and the thinly scattered law-enforcement personnel all weakened efforts to control crime. Indeed, rates of many types of deviance have always been lowest in the eastern states, especially in New England, and highest in the Far West, according to both official statistics and journalistic impressions. The latter apply especially to many types of deviant performance and belief, such as the "hippie" cult and exotic religions. Available statistics summarized in Table 1 show that regional differences vary markedly with types of deviance. In considering these figures, however, it is important to raise questions

Table 1
Rates of Deviance by Region Within the United States
(per 100,000 population per year)

Type of deviance (and basis of rate)	New England	Middle Atlantic	North Central	South	Mountain	Pacific
Predation (crimes known to police)[a]						
Burglary	921	1,005	807	837	1,030	1,563
Theft of $50 or more (non-auto)	637	777	654	616	952	1,226
Auto theft	609	501	416	308	384	606
Aggravated assault	75	139	122	187	141	188
Robbery	66	227	149	112	78	175
Forcible rape	9	14	17	17	21	32
Nonnegligent homicide	3	6	6	10	5	6
Deviant performance[b]						
Mental Illness (first admissions to public mental hospitals)	123	100	73	84	64	67
Suicides[c]	9	8	9	10	14	17

[a] Types of predation are arranged in sequence from highest to lowest rates nationally (FBI, 1970: Table 3). Unfortunately, regional data are only available on these seven so-called Index crimes.

[b] Computed from U.S. Department of Health, Education and Welfare, 1969a: Table 4, with regional groupings of states and their estimated 1967 population taken from FBI Uniform Crime Reports for that year. Mental hospital admission data were not available for some states, however, so regional rates were calculated using only the population for the states with hospital data. States omitted were Massachusetts in the New England region, Indiana in the North Central region and Idaho in the Mountain region.

[c] Computed from U.S. Department of Health, Education and Welfare, 1969b: Table 7-7, with regional groupings of states and their estimated 1967 populations taken from FBI Uniform Crime Reports for that year.

on the validity of statistics on deviance, which we discussed in the preceding chapter.

The routinely available deviance statistics are exclusively from government agencies, so their accuracy is a function of the relationship of the government to persons involved in deviance. Acts of predation have definite victims whom one expects to be motivated to report to the police. Therefore, one might presume that tabulations of the number of crimes known to the police include precise data on the volume of predation. In reality, however, this is often severely limited by a reluctance of victims to report. Most rape and some assault and fraud are not reported to the police because they are humiliating to the victims. Burglary and small-scale theft and robbery are often not reported because the victim is not aware of his losses, does not know their source, has little confidence in the ability of the police to solve the crime, does not wish to take the time that may be required of him as a complainant in the prosecution, or knows the offender and does not wish to prosecute. Even after these acts are reported, statistics are often rendered inaccurate by poor police recording and incomplete tabulation, because of inefficiency or fear of adverse public reaction to the police if crimes reported greatly exceed crimes solved. Statistics on nonpredatory types of deviance are especially incomplete because they only cover the acts government officials either encounter on their own initiative or hear about from an audience that is not victimized, and may be either not well informed or not highly motivated to report. This applies to deviant selling, such as prostitution and narcotics peddling, as well as to most types of deviant consumption and performance, such as gambling and mental illness (Glaser, 1967).

Examining Table 1 with the foregoing limitations in mind, one can observe that Pacific Coast states have the highest rates of burglary, theft, robbery, rape, and suicide, but that auto theft is reported slightly more frequently in New England. The South's lead in assault and homicide rates suggests a lingering of frontier values there as part of a subculture in which a violent response to affront or rebuff is considered a moral obligation of manhood. On the other hand, rates of mental hospital admission have a distribution almost opposite to those of most other types of deviance, but they may partially reflect regional variations in affluence, hence willingness to expend money for hospitalization of the mentally ill. Unfortunately, little research has been directed to advancing our knowledge of the reasons for these current geographical variations in rates of deviance among major regions of the country.

There is considerable difference in the toleration of deviance among various types of community. In the crowded streets of New

York and in its parks and squares, one can see people vigorously talking and gesticulating to themselves who are completely ignored by passersby. In small cities they would probably be committed to a mental institution. On the other hand, thinly settled rural areas with little influx of new population are distinctive for retention of mental or physical defectives and the mentally ill in farm households, rather than committing them to institutions. Where these individuals have been known on a personal basis by the neighbors all their lives, an accommodation is made for their handicaps, and they are viewed more as eccentric than as deviant.[1]

Within each region frontier conditions seem to be most closely approximated in the crowded slum areas of large cities. These have long been the areas of resettlement for poor rural families and for deviants not able to settle elsewhere. The older urban poor in America have been mostly migrants who were once marginal farmers or agricultural laborers but were displaced by massive crop failures or by the mechanization of agriculture. Prior to the 1920s they came to American cities primarily from Ireland, Italy, and other parts of Europe, but after the first quarter of the twentieth century they came to the cities from rural areas of the United States, especially from the South. In the cities the poor or deviant could find dwellings readily only in neighborhoods least attractive to more settled and conforming urban residents. These neighborhoods are the slums, areas of old domiciles in transition to industrial or commercial land use, and therefore, areas in which residential structures had been allowed to deteriorate.

Interspersed with the slums, often adjacent to "exotic" restaurant and commercial amusement areas, most large cities have small "Bohemias"—colonies of artists and of others who like to be associated with artists. The artist has traditionally been viewed as a marginal person, detached from the conventional world, and

---

[1] In showing that lower class and less well-educated parents are much less willing than middle class or more educated parents to keep children of very low IQ in a mental institution, Jane R. Mercer observes: ". . . a person may be mentally retarded in one system and not mentally retarded in another. He may change his label by changing his social group" (Mercer, 1965). For a fuller analysis see Farber, 1968.

less bound than others by its standards. In some niches on the inner edge of metropolitan residential space such Bohemias are accessible but separate, and the metropolitan population's conception of artists results in their tolerating somewhat different standards of consumption, performance, and belief there than prevail in other parts of the city (for historical perspective, see Berger, 1967). The slums and Bohemias are today's frontiers, on the edges of more settled neighborhoods within cities rather than on the edges of settled vast geographical regions.

The high deviance rates in the slums have occurred not so much among the poor migrants as among their children reared there. Deviant selling is centered in the slums, though often financed and supervised from elsewhere, because this is the section of the city where such deviance is most tolerated. Certain types of illegal services, such as the numbers game and other cheap gambling, seem to have a unique clientele among the poor. The poor are more inclined to make small bets on long shots and to dream of sudden wealth than are the affluent, who can procure legal gambling services from stockbrokers. In addition, the market for drugs is centered in the slums, and users from elsewhere come there to purchase. Prostitutes and panderers, however, and sometimes bookmakers and drug dealers, go out from slums to conduct business then return to slum abodes.

In slum areas of our cities there is a high concentration not only of deviance, but also of family problems. More often in the slums than elsewhere, a child has only one parent because of death, divorce, separation, illegitimacy, or imprisonment. One or more family members may be alcoholic, addicted, or criminal. These problems give such families more straitened economic circumstances than those of other slum dwellers, making it harder for them to move, and thus contributing to their high concentration in the slums.

Slum houses have many people per room and little yard space. The street serves many of the functions here that yards, recreation rooms, and even living rooms perform in more affluent neighborhoods. Because so much of their life is on the street and so many of their families have one or both parents absent most of the time, youth in the slums are on their own at an early age to

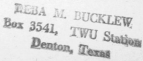

an unusual extent. They make their own moral order there, including much of conventional normative standards, but they also frequently accept much that would be deviant elsewhere. In this they differ only in degree—not absolutely—from all youth in today's society. (Suttles, 1968; Short and Strodtbeck, 1965: Chs. 3, 6, 7, 10).

REFERENCES

Berger, Bennett M.
> 1967   "Hippie morality—more old than new." trans-action 5 (December): 19–27.

Farber, Bernard
> 1968   Mental Retardation: Its Social Context and Social Consequences, Boston: Houghton, Mifflin.

Federal Bureau of Investigation, U.S. Department of Justice
> 1970   Uniform Crime Reports—1969. Washington: U.S. Government Printing Office.

Glaser, Daniel
> 1967   "National goals and indicators for the reduction of crime and delinquency." Annals of the American Academy of Political and Social Science 371 (May): 104–126.

Mercer, Jane R.
> 1965   "Social system and clinical perspective: frames of reference for understanding career patterns of persons labelled as mentally retarded." Social Problems 13 (Summer): 18–34.

Short, James F., Jr. and Fred L. Strodtbeck
> 1965   Group Process and Gang Delinquency. Chicago: University of Chicago Press.

Suttles, Gerald D.
> 1968   The Social Order of the Slum. Chicago: University of Chicago Press.

U.S. Department of Health, Education and Welfare
    1969a   Patients in State and County Mental Hospitals, 1967.
            Washington: U.S. Government Printing Office.
    1969b   Vital Statistics of the U.S. Washington: U.S. Govern-
            ment Printing Office.

3

ADOLESCENCE AND THE MARGINALITY OF THE DEVIANT

Just as the frontiers where deviance is most concentrated are on the margins of less deviant areas, the period in life during which deviance occurs most extensively is marginal to that of conventional adulthood. Adolescence is the status period intermediate between childhood and adulthood. In American society it begins when an individual is recognized as having gained distinctly more role performance capacity than a child, usually around puberty, and it terminates when the adolescent assumes all the role responsibilities of an adult, either by becoming self-supporting or, in the case of some females, by marriage. An adolescent is biologically no longer a child, but socially not accepted as an adult. His is an age of anticipating adult independence, yet living without adult responsibilities, and being often tremendously concerned about what sort of an adult he wants to be and will be.

Because of a variety of technological developments, adolescents in today's advanced industrial societies spend more and more of their hours separated from people of other age groups. Education is consolidated in large schools, with large classes in each grade, and demands on youth for collaboration with adults in family work have diminished because of such developments as the increase of labor-saving appliances in the home, more preprocessing of foods, and fewer family businesses. As a consequence of these changes, there has also been a large increase in the proportion of mothers with jobs outside the home or in much other activity away from the household when their children reach adolescence. Increased affluence in the society also means that a larger proportion of the leisure activities of adolescents in all neighborhoods are pursued in commercial and public places away from home, or in each others' homes but away from parents. All of these developments mean that the age homogeneity of school hours is extended more than ever before to the rest of the week. Indeed, adolescents now have their most separated social life outside of school, when there are many hours in which neither teachers nor parents are involved with them.[1]

In addition to being more separate, adolescence now is longer for most youth, because preparation for adult responsibilities in a technological society takes more time than formerly. In the 1960s for the first time a majority of American high school graduates entered college, including growing proportions from all social classes. More students than ever before extend their studies into graduate school. In contrast, until around 1950 more high school students dropped out than graduated, and they began adult roles as unskilled or semiskilled laborers or as apprentices to skilled tradesmen.

If we define adolescence as ending for a male when he becomes fully self-supporting, it seems safe to assert that in the middle of the twentieth century, in only a few decades, the modal age of adolescence termination for American males moved from around 16 or 17 to around 21 or 22, primarily because of the increase in years of school attendance. Since adolescence begins with puberty at around 13 years of age, one can assert that the modal duration of adolescence has doubled in this period, from about four to perhaps eight years. There has always been considerable variation around these modes.

[1] Cross-cultural and historical perspective on the trend to age homogeneity in social interaction is provided by Eisenstadt (1956). The function of generational separation in promoting deviant behavior among youth in British upper-class schools and in a variety of educational settings in technologically underdeveloped nations is interestingly detailed by Musgrove (1964). The most thorough and rigorously validated portrayal of high school students in the United States (Coleman, 1961) shows their differentiation into somewhat distinct athletic, popularity, and academic achievement oriented "crowds," each having a variant of the general adolescent subculture.

A somewhat tangential observation of possible relevance to our discussion at this point is that pubescence has occurred at a slightly earlier average age in recent years than formerly, presumably due to improved nutrition. This trend lengthens adolescence even further. In addition, it may be noted that college students, particularly those in such nonvocational curricula as the liberal arts and not employed at full-time jobs, are often an especially isolated group. Regardless of their age they are regarded neither as adults nor as adolescents by either of these two age status groups.

A fundamental law of sociology and anthropology is that social separation results in cultural differentiation. The more adolescents interact exclusively with each other, the more their customs and values become different from those of other age groups. These variations range from styles of dress, speech, music, and dancing to normative standards as to what acts or attributes make a person acceptable. Table 2 shows the relatively low age of most persons formally designated as deviant, in various ways, in American society.

Adolescence is an age of much role conflict in the United States because the borderline between it and adulthood has become especially vague here. As a result of the ambiguity in social perceptions of his status, the adolescent continually wants more of the prerogatives of adulthood than adults are willing to grant him. In particular, he wants independence in determining what work he should do and how he should spend his leisure time, while adults often expect from him more of an adult's sense of responsibility for his work than the adolescent is willing to assume. Much of the basis for this conflict is that the adolescent is interacting in both adult and adolescent social worlds, but each often has different expectations of him.[2]

Parents, teachers, and others to whom society gives power over the adolescent and an obligation to help socialize him, approve

[2] Indeed, these conflicts often begin during childhood. The legal term "incorrigible" denotes a child or adolescent (up to age 16, 17, or 18, depending on the state) who persistently disobeys adult authority. For this the juvenile court may commit him to an institution or assign him to a foster home; after the age when juvenile court authority ends, he may disobey adults as much as he likes without suffering penalties from a court, as long as he does not violate criminal law.

Table 2
Median Ages of Persons Involved in Various Types of Deviance

Type of deviance (and basis of age measurement)	Median age
Predation (age at arrest):	
Auto theft	17.3
Other theft over $50	17.6
Burglary	17.6
Robbery	19.0
Rape	22.3
Aggravated assault	26.0
Nonnegligent homicide	27.4
Forgery, counterfeiting, fraud, and embezzlement	27.5
Deviant Consumption (age at first mental hospital admission):	
Drug addiction	25.9
Alcoholism	44.9
Deviant Consumption (age at arrest):	
Narcotics[a]	19.4
Deviant Selling (age at arrest):	
Prostitution	22.9
Gambling[b]	39.7
Deviant Performance (age at first mental hospital admission):	
Mental deficiency	24.2
Schizophrenia	32.2
Deviant Performance (age at arrest):	
Running away	15.4
Disorderly conduct	23.2
Vagrancy	27.9
Drunkenness	41.7
Suicide (age at death):	48.3

[a] Includes some arrests for selling or for possession ostensibly to sell, but most arrests are for possession presumably for consumption, and most involve nonaddictive drugs, primarily marijuana.

[b] Includes some arrests for consuming illegal services, but mostly for selling.

Sources: For ages at arrest, FBI, 1970: Table 27.
For ages at hospitalization, U.S. Dept. of H.E.W., 1969a: Table 4.
For ages at death, U.S. Dept. of H.E.W., 1969b: Table 7.5.

that adolescent behavior which conforms to adult standards. To the extent that the adolescent sees himself in anticipatory socialization for their type of adulthood, he shares these standards and seeks to emulate their behavior. However, to the extent that he does not anticipate gratification from such conformity, and it involves discomfort or deprivation, he is prone to rebel. This is often manifested in acts that flout authority, such as vandalism of school property, consumption of prohibited drugs, and adoption of the opposite of required standards of dress and hairstyle. Arthur J. Stinchcombe (1964) found extensive statistical evidence that all types of misconduct in high school are associated with incompatibility between school demands and student anticipations of their future status. For example, disregard for school standards was most frequent among those students who thought their future employment would be manual, those whose grades were most below the expectations of their parents, and, in the case of girls, those who expected to be married before their eighteenth birthday.

An adolescent experiences role conflict whenever the same behavior on his part will not please both his peers and the adults with whom he interacts. Robert K. Merton (1957: 371–380) has classified a variety of mechanisms for coping with conflict in such a role set. The most conspicuous mechanism employed by adolescents is the insulation of their conformity with peer expectations from observability by adults who regard it as deviant. But living a separate life because of cultural differences creates still greater cultural contrasts, and hence a greater need to keep activity unobservable by adults. Thus an adolescent's secreting from adults behavior approved only by his peers readily initiates a dialectical progression both in this separation, and in the degree of difference between his cultural norms and those of adults.

Some statistical indices of this separation of adolescent from adult social worlds are provided in Table 3, on the age differences in rates of awareness of various types of drug usage in New York state. This shows that 17–19 year olds have first-hand knowledge of drug use many times as often as do the middle-aged people who make decisions about drug policy. No other variable—such as urban versus rural residence, race, neighborhood, education, or income—differentiates rates of awareness of drug usage nearly as much as age does. This is the generation gap made manifest. Age is more closely related than class or other variables to the rates of many other types of deviance, including most types of predation.

Because adolescents try to keep secret the behavior which adults regard as deviant, they develop many seclusive meeting

Table 3
Percentage of New York State Population Personally Knowing Someone Who Used Various Types of Drugs in the Past Year, by Age Group

Drug	Age group						Ratio of 17–19 to 50 and over rates
	13 to 16	17 to 19	20 to 29	30 to 39	40 to 49	50 and over	
Marijuana	30.7	50.5	28.0	13.4	11.1	4.4	11.5
LSD	11.9	20.8	13.4	4.9	2.9	1.6	13.0
Methedrine ("Speed")	7.5	17.4	7.7	1.9	2.7	0.8	21.8
Other amphetamines ("pep pills")	12.2	22.8	10.7	5.1	4.5	1.2	19.0
Barbiturates ("sleeping pills")	6.3	13.0	6.1	2.8	2.6	1.0	13.0
Glue sniffing	14.6	16.5	5.9	2.8	2.9	1.4	11.8
Heroin	8.6	17.1	8.1	5.1	3.3	2.3	7.4

Source: From a survey of a representative sample of New York State residents aged 13 and over, conducted by Audits and Surveys, Inc., late in 1968 for the New York State Narcotic Addiction Control Commission, and reported in Glaser and Snow, 1969.

places and hangouts, and have periodic special gatherings. At such locales there can be a safer conformity to norms, such as some on drug use, which define desirable behavior to many youth but deviant conduct to adults. San Francisco's Haight-Asbury district, Chicago's Old Town, and New York's East Village have gained national reputations as such meeting places, as did Woodstock for a single episodic gathering of an estimated 300,000 youth in 1969. Innumerable other places exist, but each is known only locally. A special "underground" press has developed that caters to the interests and tastes distinguishing such youth subcultures. There are, of course, older participants in these centers and gatherings, both those who share the standards more prevalent among adolescents, and those attracted by the commercial opportunities of this youth market.

As already implied, social isolation from adults also fosters resolution of role conflict by what Merton (1957: 377) calls "the mechanism of special support by others in similar social statuses with similar problems of coping with an unintegrated role set." Standards of expertise, daring, or other achievement in deviant activities shared by peers provide youth with an opportunity to obtain from deviance recognition, esteem, and a sense of their own competence. Social support by peers for deviant achievement begins with delinquent activity in childhood, continues in young adolescent gangs or cliques, and is extended over a wide span of years in social circles which cultivate connoisseurship in crime, drug consumption, homosexuality, or other types of deviance. These are especially attractive to those who are both successful at them and unsuccessful at conventional pursuits or unaccepted in nondeviant circles.

Many adolescents and adults can effectively segment their lives, so that their deviant activity is not known in their own social circles where it would be disapproved. They may thus maintain acceptability to both deviant and conventional associates. However, it is for the person who is unsuccessful or rejected in conventional pursuits, that deviance offers especially appealing alternative pathways to self-esteem. Furthermore, a major source of failure in conventional pursuits is the time, energy, and cost of deviant activities—from chronic alcoholism to homosexuality—as well as the exposure and disgrace that are its occasional consequences. Rates of failure in conventional pursuits are higher for slum youth than for those in better residential areas because of the former's lesser home facilities and poorer models for achievement in school; conversely, opportunities and models for deviance are more often encountered in the slums than elsewhere.

Pursuit of status in deviant activities, especially in adolescence, operates as what Norbert Wiley (1967) calls a "mobility trap." It provides immediate status gains through the recognition it elicits from peers, but these gains as an adolescent may lead to long-run social mobility blockage as an adult, due to such consequences of deviance as expulsion from school, a criminal record, and other aspects of stigma in the conventional world. Many intelligent and energetic persons with leadership potential are trapped at lower-status jobs because adolescent deviance prevented their obtaining the educational qualifications and the nondeviant character record needed for executive and professional careers. An alternative to this trap is to remain in a deviant career.

REFERENCES

Coleman, James S.
  1961   The Adolescent Society. New York: Free Press.
Eisenstadt, S. D.
  1956   From Generation to Generation. New York: Free Press.
Federal Bureau of Investigation, U.S. Department of Justice
  1970   Uniform Crime Reports—1969. Washington: U.S. Government Printing Office.
Glaser, Daniel, and Mary Snow
  1969   Public Knowledge and Attitudes on Drug Abuse in New York State. Albany, N.Y.: New York State Narcotic Addiction Control Commission.
Merton, Robert K.
  1957   Social Theory and Social Structure, Rev. ed. New York: Free Press.
Musgrove, F.
  1964   Youth and the Social Order. London: Routledge and Kegan Paul.
Stinchcombe, Arthur J.
  1964   Rebellion in a High School. Chicago: Quadrangle Books.
U.S. Department of Health, Education and Welfare
  1969a   Patients in State and County Mental Hospitals, 1967. Washington: U.S. Government Printing Office.
  1969b   Vital Statistics of the U.S.—1967. Washington: U.S. Government Printing Office.
Wiley, Norbert
  1967   "The ethnic mobility trap and stratification theory." Social Problems 15 (Fall): 147–159.

4

THE DIFFERENTIAL DEVELOPMENT OF DEVIANT CAREERS

Journalists, sociologists, and others frequently describe causes of deviance as though their effects were always cumulative and irreversible. Such explanations imply that anyone starting to engage in deviance will pursue it increasingly thereafter. However, any systematic observation of representative samples of the population almost anywhere soon reveals that such a view is grossly inaccurate. Just about everyone has at some time engaged in behavior generally regarded as deviant, but in the life histories of most people, discontinuities and reversals of trend seem as numerous as linear progressions in deviance.

Of course, there are many sources of growth in deviance. It is a fundamental principle of psychology that behavior that is gratifying—or, in psychological terms, reinforced—tends to be repeated. Some types of crime are not only immediately rewarding, but are least often solved by the police—crimes such as theft, burglary, and forgery. Those who commit them tend to be the most persistent in their offenses. Yet the follow-up studies available, and the low median age of these offenders, suggest that most of them reform eventually.

Edwin M. Lemert (1951; 1967: Chapter 3) coined the term secondary deviance to refer to an increase or change in deviance that is not a consequence of the gratifications it yields directly, but of the reactions of others to it.[1] Mechanisms of secondary deviance production are diverse. One example is that of the misbehaving child who finds companionship and praise for his conduct only from "bad" children, because after his initial or "primary" deviance he is excluded from play with "good" children. Another example is the youth committed to a state training school for minor theft who is seduced or coerced into homosexuality there, in addition to learning new predatory values and skills. A somewhat different secondary deviance development occurs when experimentation with narcotics leads to addiction, and therefore to a need for more drugs than legitimate income can support, forcing the drug user into theft or prostitution to pay for narcotics.

In recent sociological literature the most cited mechanism of secondary deviance production is labelling. The person labelled by others as a thief, a homosexual, a "dope fiend," or other type of deviant may accept this label for himself because of the effects of suggestion or persuasion, or because of the acceptance and support of others similarly labelled. The label may give him new friends, at the same time that it results in rejection by old ones. Thus one way of coping with a derogatory label is often to justify it to oneself and others, and consequently, to act more than ever in a manner that validates the label. A reputation as deviant is often an unavoidable consequence of arrest, public accusation, trial, conviction, or simply gossip, so these may promote secondary deviance. Much criminal court procedure has been described as a degradation ceremony, deliberately designed to define a person as deviant in his own mind and in the minds of others (Garfinkel, 1956). Being labelled a deviant may thus reduce either the opportunity or the desire to avoid deviance, or both.

It should be stressed, nevertheless, that secondary deviance is not a uniform consequence of labelling. It is one of at least three courses of behavior that can be distinguished as alternative reactions to being publicly designated a deviant, and all three types

---

[1] In his original formulation, Lemert (1951: 76) succinctly defined secondary deviance: "When a person begins to employ his deviant behavior or a role based upon it as a means of defense, attack or adjustment to the overt and covert problems created by the consequent societal reaction to him, his deviation is secondary."

occur frequently. Perhaps the most common mode of reaction is to try to change one's behavior so as to avoid or lose a deviant reputation. This mode occurs if people are deterred from further deviance as a result of being humiliated or punished for primary deviance. That this is probably the most frequent reaction to labelling can be inferred from several sources. For example, questionnaires have repeatedly shown that most adults admit committing considerable delinquency in their youth, such as petty shoplifting, which they subsequently cease (Wallerstein and Wyle, 1947; Porterfield, 1946; Erickson and Empey, 1963). Probing that I have done in conjunction with such inquiries almost invariably reveals that the turning point was some traumatic experience of being caught or becoming afraid of being caught and labelled for these activities. A systematic study also has shown that rigid avoidance of further deviance after being caught once is the reaction predominant among nonprofessional—though often long previously persistent—shoplifters. Once apprehended they become preoccupied with hiding or disproving the deviant label, in part by avoiding further shoplifting (Cameron, 1964).

The principal factor involved in reaction to a deviant label by conformity to the dominant norms rather than by further deviance seems to be what Jackson Toby has called "stake in conformity." [2] As indicated in discussing the role conflicts of ado-

[2] The tendency to react to labelling either by hyperconformity or by hyperdeviance was analyzed by Parsons (1951: Chapter 7) as the result of a sequential process involving: first, frustration from norm conformity generating ambivalence, either toward the norms or toward persons whose response to conformity has been frustrating; second, coping with this ambivalence either by repressing it and becoming hyperconforming in compensation, or by being more nonconforming and hence, by a vicious circle, increasingly frustrated and alienated toward the norms or toward the persons who represent them; third, being either active or passive in these reactions, according to one's personality or circumstances. These three sequential dichotomies generate eight types of deviance. Active hyperconformity to norms involves (1) compulsive norm enforcement or (2) compulsive domination of others, while passive hyperconformity involves (3) perfectionism or (4) hypersubmissiveness. Hyperalienation in its active forms involves (5) compulsive aggressiveness or (6) incorrigibility or, in its passive form, (7) compulsive independence from others or (8) com-

lescence, most people segment their lives to some degree, so that behavior acceptable in some of their social circles but not in others is only exhibited where acceptable. Adolescence is a high point of deviance initiation because so much of it is spent by small groups of peers in isolation from adults; involvement in deviance usually tapers rapidly when the adolescent mingles more with adults, in work and marriage. These family and job commitments are expressed most vigorously by those caught in deviant acts who try to keep their "disgrace" secret from family or employers, and beg for another chance, which they usually do not abuse. It is such stake in conformity, for it means acceptance by the dominant groups in society, which accounts for the 80 percent and higher success rates of probation for adults convicted of serious crime (England, 1957). Labelling indicates a failure in the segmentation of their deviant and conforming lives, which they correct by terminating some deviant activities.

Enhancement of deviance is a second, quite opposite, and probably less frequent reaction to labelling. It is characteristic of those who have a stake in *non*conformity, or who acquire such a stake as a consequence of labelling. This is perhaps best exemplified in the area of beliefs, for champions of deviant religious and political faiths are probably the deviants who are most gratified by publicity. Public labelling gives them a sense of importance that may make their stake in nonconformity much greater than it was when they were only part of a less well-known political or religious movement. Labelling may also enhance the stake in nonconformity of delinquents if it changes them from "punks" to "big shots" in what they perceive as the views of their peers; this occurs especially when they have little family or school reinforcement as "good boys" to give them a stake in conformity that being labelled delinquent might jeopardize, or when they can hide their delinquency from family or from school officials. Even an osten-

---

pulsive evasion of norms. Like most typologies in the social sciences, this eight-category unfolding oversimplifies reality in order to clarify its major dimensions, and it has not been systematically investigated, but illustrative cases of all eight patterns are not difficult to find. One of the most thorough analyses of the differentiation of youth into conforming or deviant commitments is Briar and Piliavin (1965).

sibly derogatory label may increase the attention given people who were previously ignored, and so may be gratifying to them, but only if they have no offsetting loss of valued social relationships or self-conceptions as a result of the label.

Many deviants never identified with each other or felt a sense of unity until opponents labelled them collectively, and thus gave them a sense of their numbers, their common features, and their need to organize and to coordinate for their common defense. That conflict unifies a group is a sociological law, though not without qualifications to account for exceptions (and the qualifications have not yet been adequately specified). In defensive reaction to stigma from labelling, homosexuals have developed their own societies and magazines to proclaim the right to homophily, diverse delinquent cliques have integrated into formal gangs or federations of gangs, and some scattered groups of "heretics" or "malcontents" have become large religious or political movements and ultimately new denominations, new religions, or new political parties.

A third alternative mode of reaction to labelling is that of equivocation and counter-labelling, which Gresham Sykes and David Matza (1957, 1961) call "neutralization," John Lofland (1969) calls "conventionalization," and Sigmund Freud called "rationalization." This defense against labelling consists of redefining the deviance to oneself and to others as conformity, or at least as not reflecting anything seriously objectionable. Thus people ascribe their lapses from normative behavior—their drunkenness, sexual assault, or cheating, for example—to unusual stress, to mistreatment by another person, or to temporary weaknesses, or they say that their misbehavior was excusable in view of how good they have been at other times. They may also excuse their predation by derogating the victim, by claiming that their theft or the injury they inflicted was justified because of wrongs previously suffered by them, or by asserting that their offense was due to unusual provocation, that it was for a very moral purpose, or that it was never intended to hurt or deprive the victim severely. Such rationalizations are seen by many sociologists and by some psychologists not just in the Freudian sense of excuses after the deviant acts, but as thinking processes preceding the acts or simultaneous with them, and essential motivations for the acts.[3] These modes of thinking permit people both to engage in deviant behavior and to reject an identification of themselves as unacceptable persons, thus avoiding cognitive dissonance.

Rationalizations for deviance may be difficult to maintain when the deviance leads to suffering and a sense of failure or guilt, unless there is exceptionally strong support for the deviance from others, as in close-knit deviant religious sects. As indicated in our discussion of adolescents, deviance may create a "mobility trap" because its interference with conventional cultural learning and the stigma of a deviant label impede a person in legitimate occupational pursuits. Similarly, conformity to the deviant subculture may result in formation of habits directly contrasting with those needed in conventional pursuits. Thus delinquents develop modes of speech and deportment that alienate them from middleclass employers. To cite another example, homosexuals who take the role of the opposite sex have difficulty if they seek a heterosexual relationship. If deviant pursuits are persistently gratifying, however, most interest in their nondeviant alternative activities may be extinguished.

Because social separation results in cultural differentiation, deviants develop their own standards of appraisal and achievement. Narcotics users, for example, become connoisseurs of various types of drugs and styles of drug taking, with special languages as well as fads and fashions, continuously creating new opportunities for them to enhance their sense of sophistication

[3] Perhaps the most adequate formulation of this symbolic interactionist theory of motivation is still that of C. Wright Mills (1940). This theory was validated by Cressey's (1953) finding that persons in a position of trust who embezzled money did so not when they just had an unsharable financial problem for which they saw their offense as the only solution, but only—often some time later—when they also developed a verbal interpretation of the offense that made it compatible in their minds with their conceptions of themselves as good persons. Criminological application of this verbal interpretation conception of motivation was developed further by Matza (1964) and Hartung (1965: 62–83). The psychologist George Kelly (1955) independently elaborated a sophisticated theory of motivation that turns out to be largely convergent with this sociological theory.

(well illustrated in Finestone, 1957 and Fiddle, 1967). Professional criminals become specialists in various types of predation, take pride in their skills and contacts, and between arrests, support a more lavish standard of living than they could otherwise achieve (classic descriptions are found in Sutherland, 1937 and Maurer, 1940 and 1964). Persistence in crime, and hence pride in it, is most characteristic of the "safe rackets" where the risks of arrest are minimal. It is especially associated with organized deviant selling, as in the provision of illegal gambling services. Most deviant pursuits, however, involve some risk of effective repression by the dominant society, are frequently interrupted, and have considerable turnover in personnel. Furthermore, few deviants lose all stake in conformity. Indeed, the older successful criminals tend to invest in conventional businesses and strive for "respectability" in nondeviant circles.

Most people are inconsistent with respect to deviance both in brief periods and over the course of their lifetime. Studies of the careers of cross-sections of criminal, alcoholic, drug-addicted and other types of deviants repeatedly reveal a cyclical pattern. This is quite apart from their diverse reactions to labelling. During a period of gratification in deviant activity they become committed to it, but when deviance leads to unusual stress they reduce or cease their involvement in it, and perhaps respond to efforts of others to resocialize them to conformity. Subsequently they revert to their deviance again during a period of stress in their pursuit of a conforming career. Thus alcoholics and drug addicts become abstinent for a period after they "hit bottom," as they put it. Often they are aided at that critical time by Alcoholics Anonymous, by an ex-addict group, or by other therapeutic agents, and this is the only time they are voluntarily very cooperative with those who aid them. Permanent cures are the exception rather than the rule, however, and most of those endeavoring to alter such compulsive deviant consumption recognize that change in such deviance usually occurs not abruptly and permanently but by gradual dampening of the oscillation cycle (Ray, 1961). Similarly, studies have shown that the vast majority of released prison inmates make some effort to "go straight" after each release from incarceration, but large proportions eventually recidivate; they follow a "zig-zag path" from crime to legitimate employment to crime and "straight" again, with most eventually abandoning efforts to make their livelihood from crime (Glaser, 1969: Chapter 17).

Deviance, as we have indicated, occurs most frequently during adolescence. However, it may also recur after periods of sustained pursuit of nondeviant adult roles, particularly when loss of job or spouse, or other tragedy, failure, or loneliness in a conforming life builds up stress beyond an individual's limits of endurance. Recidivism in crime, relapse to alcohol or drug use, and other turning points from conformity back to deviance—and occasionally even initial deviance after a lifetime with no markedly nonnormative behavior—seem to be associated with such stress, although the "limits of endurance" vary from one individual to the next. When adolescent deviance involved conflict with parents, adult relapse to deviance frequently seems to involve, during a period of stress, a recapitulation of adolescent efforts to express independence and even defiance of parents, or of spouses who become parent surrogates.

While change and persistence mechanisms in deviant careers have been illustrated here by examples from many varieties of deviance, it is obvious that their development differs somewhat according to type of deviance. Suicide, of course, is unique; it is not a career but an event. However, the mental experiences leading up to the decision to commit suicide, or a sequence of unsuccessful attempts at suicide, might be described as a career. Yet, as Ronald W. Maris (1969) and others have pointed out, those who persistently attempt suicide and those who complete it have different characteristics, which may explain why efforts to reduce suicide rates by counseling the attempters have not changed the rates. The attempters are more often female, more often in good physical health, and of a younger average age, than those who succeed in destroying themselves. There is still much diversity in suicide, and considerable overlap between attempters and succeeders in all measurable traits. What seems usually to be involved is a loss of hope for satisfying social relationships and self-conceptions that develops over a protracted span of time, and is aggravated by combinations of such conditions as social isolation, failure in endeavors, physical debilitation, guilt, unrealistic standards for oneself, and mistrust of others. Social science has gained some precision in predicting the development of suicide only in terms of the statistical rates for various groups, rather than prospects for individual cases.

A vast diversity of patterning in suicide rates has been reduced by theoretical interpretation of statistical data to a limited number of principal factors. This began with a classic in sociological research, Emile Durkheim's *Suicide* (1951), first published in 1897, which distinguished four types of suicide on the basis of the correlation of rates with what were inferred to be indicators of four different social conditions. *Egoistic* suicide rates were said to vary inversely with the degree of integration of social groups on the basis of such evidence as the higher suicide rates of unmarried than married persons, the greater suicide rates of Protestants than Catholics, and the decline of suicide in wartime. *Altruistic* suicide, however, was ascribed to a degree of integration strong enough to eliminate individuation, as in groups which successfully prescribe self-destruction for military objectives, or to relieve others of supporting one in old age or in widowhood. *Anomic* suicide was identified with a weakening of norms to regulate an individual's life, as in the rise of suicide with business failure or sudden business prosperity, and in the correlation of suicide with divorce rates. *Fatalistic* suicide was a residual category identified with an extreme degree of regulation, as in the suicide of a slave on the death of his master.

Barclay Johnson (1965) has argued that Durkheim's altruistic and fatalistic suicides are rare and that social integration and regulation are difficult to distinguish, so Durkheim really reduced suicide rates to one condition. This condition seems to be what Jack P. Gibbs and Walter T. Martin (1964) designate as "the stability and durability of social relationships within the population." By a series of rigorous logical steps, but based on postulations that are not all conclusively validated, Gibbs and Martin deduce from this that suicide will vary inversely with what they call status integration, or the extent to which the multiple statuses of people involve roles that customarily go together in their society. Thus, being 35, female, married, and a mother is a more frequent—hence, what they call integrated—combination of statuses in our society than being 15, married, female, and a mother, or being 35, single, female, and a mother, or being 35, female, married, and not a mother. Their mathematical index system provides a quantitative score for the integration of any combination of statuses for which data on frequency of all combinations is available in a society, and this index has impressive negative correlations with suicide. Though their work has been criticized, it has also been brilliantly defended by Gibbs (1969), and it seems to gain support with each increment of data that test it. There is some evidence that lack of status integration is conducive not just to suicide, but to all types of deviance, although this has not yet been well investigated.

To summarize, deviant careers generally develop in a non-linear and not easily predictable manner. Like all other behavior, deviance that is gratifying tends to be continued, and that which is not gratifying is extinguished. Physical attributes regarded as deviant, of course, are an exception to this, since they are unalterable in most instances; they can only be made more tolerable either by the persons with deviant attributes forming their own social systems, or by their successful efforts to promote tolerance by nondeviants and to achieve social integration in the dominant society. This may be a long and painful process for the deviant. Midgets, amputees, and others with such attributes, like members of minority ethnic groups, have tried both self-segregation and persistent efforts at integration, with variable gratification in each.

The labelling reactions to deviance, we noted, may generate the much cited reaction of secondary deviance, but they may also evoke a vigorous effort by the actor to salvage his stake in conformity, or his equivocation, to make deviance and conformity compatible. For all deviant behavior except suicide, appreciable effort at social control has been made by those dominant in American society, generally not guided by much knowledge of the differential development of deviant careers, and with very frequent failure to control.

REFERENCES

Briar, Scott, and Irving Piliavin
1965 "Delinquency, situational inducements, and commitment to conformity." Social Problems 13 (Summer): 34–45.
Cameron, Mary O.
1964 The Booster and the Snitch. New York: Free Press.
Cressey, Donald R.
1953 Other People's Money. New York: Free Press.
England, Ralph W., Jr.
1957 "What is responsible for satisfactory probation and post-probation outcome?" Journal of Criminal Law, Criminology and Police Science 47 (March–April): 667–676.
Erickson, Maynard L., and LaMar T. Empey
1963 "Court records, undetected delinquency and decision-making." Journal of Criminal Law, Criminology and Police Science 54 (December): 456–469.
Durkheim, Emile
1951 Suicide. John A. Spaulding and George Simpson, transl. New York: Free Press.
Fiddle, Seymour
1967 Portraits From a Shooting Gallery. New York: Harper and Row.
Finestone, Harold
1957 "Cats, kicks and color." Social Problems 5 (July): 3–13.
Garfinkel, Harold
1956 "Conditions of successful degradation ceremonies." American Journal of Sociology 61 (March): 420–424.
Gibbs, Jack P.
1969 "Marital status and suicide in the United States: a special test of the status integration theory." American Journal of Sociology 74 (March): 521–533.
Gibbs, Jack P., and Walter T. Martin
1964 Status Integration and Suicide. Eugene, Ore.: University of Oregon Press.

Glaser, Daniel
  1969   The Effectiveness of a Prison and Parole System. Rev.
          ed. Indianapolis: Bobbs-Merrill.
Hartung, Frank E.
  1965   Crime, Law and Society. Detroit: Wayne State Uni-
          versity Press.
Johnson, Barclay D.
  1965   "Durkheim's one cause of suicide," American Socio-
          logical Review 30 (December): 875–886.
Kelly, George A.
  1955   The Psychology of Personal Constructs. 2 vols. New
          York: Norton.
Lemert, Edwin M.
  1951   Social Pathology. New York: McGraw-Hill.
  1967   Human Deviance, Social Problems and Social Control.
          Englewood Cliffs, N.J.: Prentice-Hall.
Lofland, John
  1969   Deviance and Identity. Englewood Cliffs, N.J.: Prentice-
          Hall.
Maris, Ronald W.
  1969   "The sociology of suicide prevention: policy implications
          of differences between suicidal patients and completed
          suicides." Social Problems 17 (Summer): 132–149.
Matza, David
  1964   Delinquency and Drift. New York: Wiley.
Matza, David, and Gresham M. Sykes
  1961   "Juvenile delinquency and subterranean values." Ameri-
          can Sociological Review 26 (October): 712–719.
Maurer, David W.
  1940   The Big Con. Indianapolis: Bobbs-Merrill.
  1964   Whiz Mob. New Haven: College and University Press.
Mills, C. Wright
  1940   "Situated actions and vocabularies of motive," Ameri-
          can Sociological Review 5 (December): 904–913. Re-
          printed 1963 as Chapter 3 of Part 4 in Irving L. Horo-
          witz (ed.), *Power,* Politics and People: The Collected
          Essays of C. Wright Mills. New York: Ballantine Books.
Parsons, Talcott
  1951   The Social System. New York: Free Press.

Porterfield, Austin L.
  1946   Youth in Trouble. Austin, Tex.: Leo Potishman Foundation.
Ray, Marsh
  1961   "The cycle of abstinence and relapse among heroin addicts." Social Problems 9 (Fall): 132–140.
Sutherland, Edwin H.
  1937   The Professional Thief. Chicago: University of Chicago Press.
Sykes, Gresham M., and David Matza
  1957   "Techniques of neutralization." American Sociological Review (December): 664–670.
Toby, Jackson
  1957   "Social disorganization and stake in conformity: complementary factors in the predatory behavior of hoodlums." Journal of Criminal Law, Criminology and Police Science 48 (June): 12–17.
Wallerstein, James S., and Wyle, Clement J.
  1947   "Our law-abiding lawbreakers." Probation 25 (March–April): 107–112, 118.

5

SOCIAL CONTROL OF DEVIANCE

Objectives in the control of deviance can be described by six "Rs": revenge, rejection, repression, restraint, rehabilitation, and reintegration. The first three "Rs" are most applicable to former periods in western societies and the last three to modern times, though none of these objectives has ever been completely absent, for all types of deviance, anywhere. The last two, rehabilitation and reintegration, often refer much more to hopes than to accomplishments, and none of the six is always discrete, for some social control measures are aimed at two or more of these objectives simultaneously. Nevertheless, these six headings aid in bringing order to analysis of the vast variety of activity that has been directed at the social control of deviance. It should be remembered throughout this section that the discussion is of the methods that dominant groups may use to control what they regard as deviance, and of their differential effectiveness for such control, apart from the question of the merits and consequences of defining various behavior or attributes as deviant. The latter topic is the concern of our final chapter.

REVENGE

The traditional—so-called normal—reaction to predation is to seek vengeance. The victim and his family or friends try to injure the predator. Often revenge is sought not just against the offender, but also against any of his family or other associates that can be victimized, and these then seek counter-revenge. As a consequence feuds develop between families, gangs, tribes, or even nations, with members of each reciprocally assaulting, stealing, or vandalizing against members of the others so often that the original predatory act that initiated the feud is completely forgotten.

Such conflict is so disruptive within any society that a major function of societal leadership is always the social control of predation. This is done by regarding serious predation against any member of the society as an offense against the whole. Therefore, societal leadership inflicts punishment on the predator and prohibits its being done by the predator's victim or his supporters. It should be noted that state punishment serves five somewhat separate interests. The first is to satisfy the passions of the victims of predation and their sympathizers. The second is to achieve so-called transcendental justice, to balance each wrong with a penalty as a matter of abstract religious or philosophical principle. The third is for individual deterrence, to make the offender afraid to repeat his deviance. The fourth is for general deterrence, to make the rest of the population fearful of punishment should they engage in the deviance. The fifth is to define the deviance as disapproved by the state (even if it is only punished in a minute proportion of cases, as for example, adultery, which is a crime in most states). Each of these five interests has somewhat different implications in deciding what penalty the state should impose, and each has greatly concerned legal philosophers and theorists for centuries.

Revenge-taking in pure form, with none of the other five "Rs" involved, survives as a frequent and official government action only in the levying of fines, since corporal punishment by the state has virtually disappeared, and during the 1960s capital punishment dwindled to a few executions per year and finally to none. Of course, these and other punitive actions sometimes are taken by the public or the police without court authorization.

The similarity of homicide rates in adjacent states with and without capital punishment, and within states before and after termination of capital punishment, indicate that this attempt at general deterrence—as compared with the alternative of long-term imprisonment—is largely irrelevant in affecting the occurrence of murder. Its more frequent use in regions with high homicide rates, such as the southeastern states, suggests that both murder and the death penalty reflect mostly the extent to which there exists a subculture in which killing is considered a morally obligatory response to a large range of rebuff or disagreement, outweighing the moral tenet that all life is sacred. Thus the main function of capital punishment appears to be to satisfy the emotions of the public and their abstract belief in the ethic of compensating guilt by punishment. The subculture of violence not only seems to vary in regional distribution, but also in age groups within regions, with lethal assault rates at a peak among those between 20 and 30 years old. Apparently the increase in the proportion of the population in this age range and the increased prevalence of firearms in the community were the primary factors in the upturn of homicide rates in the 1960s, following decades of decline (Wolfgang and Ferracuti, 1967; Newton and Zimring, 1969; Glaser, 1970a).

Revenge by fining is a little studied—but for some deviance, apparently a highly effective—form of social control. William J. Chambliss (1967) argues that punishment is effective for individual or general deterrence only with deviance that has two characteristics: (1) it serves an *instrumental* function for the deviant, that is, it is pursued deliberately and rationally as a means to some other end, such as procuring money or saving effort, rather than as an end in itself, for expression of emotion or belief; (2) the deviant has a *low commitment* to it, that is, it is not very difficult for him to manage without it. Chambliss showed that fines were effective in reducing one such form of minor deviance, illegal parking. He argues that penalties are less effective in reducing instrumental deviance to which there is a high commitment (for example, the predations of a professional thief), more effective in reducing expressive deviance of low commitment (most rape), and least effective with expressive deviance of high commitment (drug addiction).

The Chambliss thesis is supported by reports of the reduction of street solicitation by prostitutes in Britain through fines that made it unprofitable (Walker, 1965: 241–242), although this probably did not deter them from their deviant selling off the street. It is also supported by studies showing that fines failed to alter rates of public drunkenness in Sweden (Toernudd, 1968), but that use of the "breathalyzer" by British traffic police clearly reduced driving by those who drank (Ross *et al.,* 1970). Scandinavian professors frequently relate to American visitors that they stopped even trying to drive home from parties and took taxis instead, after mandatory jail sentences were imposed for drunken driving; the driving, of course, is an instrumental act, while drunkenness alone is expressive. The Chambliss thesis is supported further by the fact that parole violation and recidivism rates, regardless of length of imprisonment, generally are low for rapists and murderers, but high for drug addicts, alcoholic forgers, child molesters, and habitual petty thieves (Glaser and O'Leary, 1966; Jacks, 1967).

Charles R. Tittle (1969), using data for the separate states, shows that certainty of punishment, as measured by ratio of persons imprisoned to crimes known to the police, varies inversely with the crime rate. He also demonstrates that severity of punishment has little relationship to the crime rate, and such correlation as it has is always positive, whether measuring severity by mean time served per imprisonment, by median length of maximum sentence, or by number of offenses subject to capital punishment. Furthermore, this relationship of certainty to lower crime rates is most marked with urbanization, but the relationship of severity to higher crime rates disappears in the most urbanized states. Although these data suggest causation of crime rates by punishment policy, we cannot be certain of the causal priority of these two variables, and cannot control enough other possibly causal variables to warrant certainty from this study alone.

Revenge presumably has a negative social control effect, when used in a manner which is not only nondeterrent by the Chambliss analysis, but also increases deviance-producing conditions. This may occur when persons who commit property crimes only during periods of extreme economic stress are rendered unemployable by incarceration or are severely fined. Measures designed to avoid this include probation rather than imprisonment for first or occasional offenders (in conjunction with restitution to victims), jailing on evenings or weekends only, making fines a percentage of average weekly earnings rather than a fixed sum for rich or poor, and allowing installment payment of fines.

Revenge against deviant groups often gives them a sense of unity, especially when they conceive of themselves as in conflict with unjust authorities. Such effects were often reported in the 1960s and 1970s following police harassment of some motorcycle gangs and black militant groups for their alleged violence and other deviance. Even more conducive to deviance, however, is indiscriminate revenge against nondeviants and deviants alike, for this converts nondeviants to deviance. This was repeatedly evident on college campuses in the 1960s and 1970s when police or National Guardsmen attacked, gassed, or prodded students quite unselectively (and often college staff, visitors, and neighbors as well) in overreacting to actual or alleged predation or illegal performance by a few students.

REJECTION

Perhaps even more universal than desire for revenge, hence "normal" as a reaction to deviance, is avoidance or expulsion. This applies to all persons considered deviant, not just predators. Rejection varies from informal avoidance to formal expulsion, exile, blacklisting, and other procedures. The formal penalty of exile today surviving in the United States is deportation for those who are not native-born citizens. Other types of formal rejection are increasingly in violation of both verbalized and legal norms. Nevertheless, rejection of members of minority ethnic groups, ex-criminals, ex-mental hospital patients, and others pervades many settings, including work places, social clubs, housing, and casual social gatherings.

The operational definition of a person as deviant is the avoidance or rejection that he experiences from others, and this has been shown to vary somewhat independently of assertions by the others as to their acceptance or rejection of him (LaPiere, 1934; Schwartz and Skolnick, 1962; Williams, 1964). Rejection behavior has been shown to be not so much a consequence of verbalized attitudes as of unfamiliarity with the deviant, and of social constraints on accepting him in particular situations, though these three factors interact somewhat (Warner and DeFleur, 1969). As indicated in our discussion of labelling mechanisms, the trial and conviction process has been aptly analyzed by Harold Garfinkel (1956) as a public degradation ceremony designed for the formal rejection of the convicted person as though he were a lower species of human entitled to fewer rights than other persons. Linsky (1970) has shown that rejection by commitment to mental hospitals occurs most frequently in communities that are homogeneous in politics, income, and ethnicity.

As previously indicated, the consequences of rejection depend on how much the rejectee values acceptance, and how achievable it is for him. Any "stake in conformity" motivates him to avoid further deviance or to hide it more carefully, if rejected, but where he has a greater stake in deviance than in conformity, or where acceptance does not seem feasible or worth the costs it is expected to require, rejection increases commitment to deviance. This accounts for the diverse consequences of labelling a person as deviant.

Many long-standing types of rejection because of deviance appear to have diminished in the United States since midcentury, as the publicity received by all varieties of deviant in the mass media—particularly television—has greatly reduced their strangeness to most people. Urbanization and travel also have increased contact between previously rejected and rejecting components of the population. Abortion, nudity, and marijuana smoking are more widely accepted today than they were at midcentury. But while the range of behavior regarded as deviant appears to diminish, this occurs much more with deviant performance, consumption, belief, and status, than with deviant selling, suicide, and predation. Polarization of public opinion on new issues, furthermore, may create new rejection of people on the basis of their beliefs or status.

REPRESSION

Revenge and rejection are often accompanied by an effort to prevent deviant ideas from being propagated. Repression involves efforts to prevent publication, assembly, broadcasting, and demonstration by deviants and to prevent nondeviants from freely contacting deviants. Free communication is guaranteed by the First Amendment of the U.S. Constitution, and is usually much more available for deviant ideas here than in countries without political democracy. Nevertheless, whenever public opinion is highly polarized on an issue, with strong feelings about it by both the dominant group in the society and by the deviants, the latter run considerable risk of repressive action either from police, from other government officials, or from groups with opposing ideas.

In the second half of the twentieth century efforts at social control of deviant belief by repression have been most conspicuous in the United States against endeavors to increase the civil rights of minority group members, and against advocates of U.S. withdrawal from the Vietnam war. As feelings intensified, both sides in these conflicts rationalized considerable stretching of usual interpretations of the rights of the others to freedom of speech, publication, assembly, demonstration, or simply movement.

When repression of deviants on the basis of their alleged interference with the rights of others seems unwarranted or excessive, a "backlash" reaction in the general public often increases support for those repressed. This was evident in the gains achieved by Dr. Martin Luther King's civil rights movement after violence was used against it in Mississippi and Alabama; it was also apparent in the gains of the peace movement after police repression of antiwar demonstrators at the 1968 Democratic Party Convention, and after the killing of four students by National Guardsmen at Kent State University in 1970. Conversely, when usually accepted limitations of the rights of demonstration are ignored by those promoting deviant beliefs, as in random violence, property destruction or drowning out of opposition speakers, a backlash reaction alienates many actual or potential supporters of their beliefs, and impedes their gaining new support. These backlash reactions of a more moderate majority to intolerance by either extreme on many issues suggest a growth in norms of tolerance for deviant beliefs as societal complexity increases and the educational level of the population is upgraded. That tolerance is a correlate of such trends was asserted by Durkheim (1947) around 1900, and while this relationship is not continuous and universal in every country or epoch, it appears to predominate in the long run. Parsons and White (1961) argue that increased tolerance of diversity in the United States has been a consequence of the educational upgrading of its population.

Repression, to be successful, has to be nearly complete, as it has often been in totalitarian countries. A message may get most attention when it is scarce, so a little media space or time may gain more audience for a communication that supports deviance than for one that supports conformity. In addition, of course, some types of deviance titillate the population. Conspicuous in mass media coverage of deviant beliefs in the United States during the second half of the twentieth century is that, while deviant groups have less money and fewer prominent supporters than conforming groups, deviant activities are so newsworthy that they receive media coverage out of all proportion to their size and resources. Efforts to repress them by prosecution in the courts often bring advocates of deviant beliefs much more opportunity to communicate to the general public than they originally expected from the acts for which they were prosecuted.

Repression of speech has generally declined in the modern history of the United States, despite occasional escalations, as in the McCarthy era of the 1950s and in efforts to repress opposition to the Vietnam war. On the whole, what are predominantly regarded as deviant beliefs are propagated now more freely than ever. This is readily evident from the street sale of the "underground press" in major cities, and from the trend in theme and style of motion pictures and theater plays.

RESTRAINT

Physical restriction of liberty by confinement in a prison or asylum became the predominant formal measure for social control over deviants in the nineteenth century, although it had some beginnings earlier. Until the end of the eighteenth century in western Europe and in the American colonies, the state sought social control over predators and other types of deviants primarily by corporal and capital punishment, expropriation of property, repression, and exile. For major predations committed by a commoner against the nobility or clergy, and for conspicuously deviant belief, the penalty was not merely death but also torture.

With growth of the middle class in size and power, beginning in the Renaissance, continuing in the Reformation, and culminating in the Enlightenment, came increased glorification of the capacity for reason, the "inalienable rights" of all men, and the value of liberty. This set of values was powerfully propagated by such influential eighteenth-century writers as Rousseau, Voltaire, and Beccaria, resulting in early nineteenth-century reform of criminal law to make penalties: (1) a function only of the offense, not specifying qualifications according to the status of the offender or victim; (2) consist of the deprivation of liberty, that is, restraint, rather than corporal or capital punishment; (3) vary according to the presumed pleasure gained by means of the deviant act; and (4) objectionable, if deemed excessive by Bentham's "felicific calculus" of imposing pain merely outweighing the pleasure of the deviance for which the convicted person is punished (Phillipson, 1923).

Workhouses for vagrants, beggars, drunkards, and others charged with deviant performance were initiated in Europe in the seventeenth century. For predation, restraint was only imposed pending trial, sentencing, and the execution of corporal or capital punishment, or of sentence to exile, rather than as punishment per se. Prisons were primarily a nineteenth-century development. This innovation was centered in the United States, and especially in the Quaker colony of Pennsylvania. Many of their early leaders, such as George Fox and William Penn, had endured pretrial confinement in British "gaols" for their religious beliefs. This confinement with criminals made them more intimately familiar with predators than most middle- and upper-class persons, and only these classes had the franchise and much influence on government at that time.

The Pennsylvania System for the treatment of felons was initiated in the Walnut Street Jail in Philadelphia in 1790, and reached an apex with the opening of the Eastern State Penitentiary in that city in 1829. This system emphasized solitary confinement in cells, in contrast with the congregate housing of all ages and sexes in large rooms in the workhouses. It permitted communication of the offender only with staff, preachers, and selected moralistic prison visitors. A Bible was placed in each cell, food was handed in through a door too small for human passage, and later some work material was also provided. The Eastern Penitentiary even had a small walled yard for each cell in which gardening was permitted. A prisoner was blindfolded when led to his cell, to reduce prospects of communication among prisoners. It was hoped that solitary meditation and differential association only with anticriminal persons would make these prisoners penitent.

Pennsylvania prison cells were spacious, and operation of this type of prison was expensive. A competing approach developed in New York state was called the Auburn System after the prison where it was initiated. It stressed solitary confinement in small cells at night, but congregate labor in silence by day. Harsh discipline was advocated by its early leaders, including flogging. The striped suit and lock-step were also initiated, to reduce escape from outside construction work. Advocates of each system pamphleteered actively, and attracted worldwide attention. De Tocqueville, Beaumont, and other distinguished Europeans came to the United States primarily to observe these prison systems. The Pennsylvania System prevailed in western Europe, while the Auburn system predominated in the United States, though each was gradually modified by some group confinement and by diminished harshness. Neither system was ever tested rigorously for its effectiveness in changing criminals; they were evaluated primarily in terms of economic costs and consistency with current values.

It is because restraint was thought of as a form of revenge, especially for predation, that there was objection to its use for an excessive period in relation to the offense. But restraint is also a direct control; a restrained person is incapacitated for deviance, and this probably motivates much of its use, in addition to providing revenge. Incapacitation as a major motive is suggested by the fact that restraint by chains, or by confinement in pits or cages, was standard practice from ancient times to the end of the eighteenth century, for that small fraction of the mentally ill who are intractable. Asylums for their more humane storage developed in the nineteenth century, simultaneously with the emergence of the "alienist," forerunner of today's psychiatrist, who was a physician appointed to help courts identify those alleged criminals whose "insanity" presumably made them not amenable to deterrence by punishment. The replacement of custodial by therapeutic concerns came later, and as a consequence, these institutions still functioned more for secure storage than for cure in much of the twentieth century.

The main function of restraint as a social control mechanism, and often an important one, is to interrupt the reinforcement of deviance. Persons who steal, rape, or commit other deviant acts tend to repeat their behavior most readily when they are successful in it and not caught; restraint ends such success and it provides what many assume is a perfect social control, for the restrainee is either kept from engaging in deviance or is removed from the view of those who would object to him. This is most frequently a spurious control, however, for two reasons. The first is that it is only temporary, since over 99 percent of the people incarcerated in American jails or prisons, and an increasingly large majority of those hospitalized for deviance, are ultimately released. Second, this control is spurious if the conditions and consequences of restraint make for more deviance after release than when restraint began. On the other hand, it is indeed a perfect control if those released are deterred, cured, released in a manner that facilitates their integration into conforming society, or are in some other way changed so as to be no longer regarded as deviant.

Jails are the least studied but most used place of restraint for deviants in the United States. Most state and federal prison inmates and many mental hospital patients are first confined in jail, pending court hearings, and an even larger number of persons alleged to be deviant are confined exclusively in jails. Jail inmates are usually held before trial only because they cannot supply bail, and about a third of those confined after trial are restrained only because they cannot pay a fine, so poverty often determines jailing independently of deviance. Public intoxication is the most frequent basis for jailing, but since the same facilities hold both drunks and persons charged with serious felonies, jails are operated with much more concern for custodial security than is necessary for the majority of their inmates.

Public indifference to jails results in their having a national average of about one staff member to seven inmates, and these are on duty around the clock, so the ratio at any time is rarely over one to twelve, and often much less (National Council on Crime and Delinquency, 1967). Therefore, security is achieved for most jail inmates by crowding appreciable numbers into large cages—variously called bullpens, tanks, or dayrooms—which most leave only when they leave the jail (for court hearings or for complete release). Food, utensils, and other supplies are passed in and out of the cages, so the men need not be moved, and they may always be observed by guards through the bars, even when using toilet facilities. Staffing, however, does not permit continuous surveillance, and group confinement in idleness means that inmates who can dominate the others by force or threat are free to do so. Accordingly, homosexual rape and robbery or extortion of any possessions they retain or can purchase (especially cigarettes) are common experiences of those inmates who are not dominant. Schooling and work opportunities are minimal in jail, especially for pretrial prisoners, so communication of inmates is mostly with each other, and criminalization probably occurs at a greater rate in jails than anywhere else. Scandals occur periodically when an unusually articulate person is jailed, or when deaths in jail are publicized, but the scandals expose only what is an endemic condition of most jails, derived from low budgets, architectural design for group confinement, and public indifference. Reforms that change the officials in charge but leave the causal conditions unaltered rarely make an enduring difference (Glaser, 1970b).

The most notable efforts to reduce the criminalizing effects of jails are those that minimize use of these institutions. Decreased pretrial confinement has resulted from dramatic experiments by the Vera Foundation for Criminal Justice in the courts of New York City. The experiments demonstrated that many accused persons will appear in court at the time of their trial even if released without bail, especially those who have had stable residence, family ties, and employment in the community. Such release on own recognizance and reductions in bail charges have spread despite the opposition of bondsmen, who use part of their profits from bail for political contributions and lobbying. The Vera Foundation has also sponsored successful experiments with use of summons instead of arrest prior to appearance in court, and with conditional pretrial release of destitute and unskilled persons on the condition that they participate in subsidized counselling, vocational training, and employment.

The Vera Foundation, in its Bowery Project in collaboration with the Salvation Army and other organizations, has also spearheaded the use of medically oriented persons to transport street drunks to a shelter and therapeutic center if they come voluntarily, thus greatly reducing the number the police haul to jail. St. Louis pioneered use of city medical facilities for drunks instead of jails. Both of these practices are being duplicated in other cities. Reduction of posttrial jailing has resulted from greater use of probation and parole from jail, as well as from the already mentioned installment payment of fines and jailing on weekends or nights only. Additional jail reforms expand privacy, education, employment, and reintegrative outside contact opportunities for both pretrial and sentenced jail inmates, and they introduce considerable difference between various units of the jail for different types of offender. Most efforts at rehabilitation in conjunction with restraint occur in prisons, training schools, and mental hospitals, to be discussed further in the next subsection.

When accused persons are tried, the probability of their receiving probation, and even their prospects of acquittal, are much higher if they have been released pending trial—whether on bail or on recognizance—than if they have been jailed. This is interpreted by advocates of bail reform as evidence of judicial prejudice against those jailed, but it probably is more a consequence of other factors. One factor, of course, is that the same qualities that make a person a good risk for pretrial release make him statistically a good risk for probation. Nevertheless, some differences in trial outcome for released and jailed accused remain after many risk influences are statistically controlled (Zeisel, 1969). The most important source of these differences probably is the impact of jail on the tactics of prosecution and defense in pretrial bargaining. Delay favors the defense, by tiring witnesses and decreasing prosecutor interest in the case, so the person released has no motivation to plead guilty in order to terminate the negotiation of justice. A man in jail, however, especially on a misdemeanor or minor felony, is eager to plead guilty and to start serving whatever sentence he may receive in order to bring his confinement to an end. Often it is only if he pleads guilty that he is likely to receive credit for pretrial confinement in counting time served on his sentence, and frequently a plea of guilty yields a sentence identical with time already confined.

REHABILITATION

Proponents of both the Pennsylvania and Auburn systems of prison management asserted that they not only restrained their inmates, but changed them to nondeviants, an accomplishment now called "rehabilitation." Today changing the deviant is the objective most stressed in public and private programs for all types of deviance except those that are immutable, such as suicides and persons with stigmatized unchangeable biological attributes, such as midgets.

Emphasis on the goal of rehabilitation distinguished the prison for young offenders opened at Elmira, New York, in the 1870s and called a reformatory. It stressed formal education and vocational training. A "reformatory movement" spread this type of institution throughout the United States and abroad, and in the twentieth century "training schools" were established for the youngest offenders, generally committed by juvenile courts. The stress of these institutions on schooling and counselling was also introduced in prisons for older offenders. Today a prison's investment in such treatment services reflects the state system it is in more than whether or not it is named a reformatory.

Eschewal of all terms connoting an interest in revenge or restraint in favor of terms that are either neutral or imply rehabilitative concerns, distinguishes so-called progressive from traditional penal systems. Thus, corrections is the term used for the field of prison administration, correctional institution for prison, and a separate correctional institution is called a school if for younger inmates, or a treatment center, medical facility, men's colony, or simply state institution for men, if for older offenders. Obviously, restraint is imposed simultaneously with an effort to educate, counsel, and train the inmates, for as the custodially oriented staff assert, "You can't treat 'em if you can't keep 'em." Indeed, the rehabilitative services were superimposed on institutions designed primarily to restrain persons, to prevent them from engaging in deviance in the community. The purpose of prison is still promulgated officially as both rehabilitation of the inmates and protection of the general populace by restraining those thought to threaten them.

This dual purpose poses the issue of compatibility of restraint with rehabilitation. Those who are confined may be highly motivated to escape, may see staff as concerned primarily with escape prevention, and therefore, may be resistant to staff efforts at education, counselling, or psychotherapy.

Correctional staff reduce hostility of prisoners by diverse means. One way is to avoid identification with the courts that order confinement. Inmates also become aware of what probably is their main deterrent against escape, the fact that it leads to arrest and reconfinement for an even longer period. Many prefer serving out their sentence to being outside only in wanted status, afraid to contact old friends or family. Staff also employ one or more of three contrasting broad strategies for obtaining custodial security: (1) physical barriers at the perimeter of the institution grounds, such as high walls, high double fences with barbed or electrified tops, and watchtowers manned by armed guards; (2) regimentation within the institution, such as allowing inmates to move only in military lines or escorted by an officer, lining them up to be counted several times per day, and searching them and their quarters frequently; (3) social psychological strategies, such as gradually giving inmates more freedom from restrictions and surveillance—trusting them more—if they cooperate in maintaining order and custody. Also, it is often made clear to inmates that the relative freedom of all, within the institution, will be curtailed if there is serious disorder or escape by even a few. This co-opts the inmates to be concerned with guaranteeing a collective order, so that their obligations to each other as well as fear of sanctions from each other, serve the staff's custodial interests.

Some correctional leaders have postulated an inverse relationship between custodial architecture and rehabilitative effectiveness. As a consequence, many institutions are built without walls or fences and with few locks as a display of trust. Public reaction to escapes, however, so jeopardizes the job security of institutional officials, that they sometimes impose more regimentation and closer surveillance—a wall of eyes—in unfenced institutions than prevail in institutions with physical barriers on the perimeter. At other institutions with similar inmates low rates of escape or disorder prevail, regardless of the presence or absence of fences, and with little regimentation. A near-zero rather than definitely negative correlation between all custodial measures and rehabilitation is suggested by the most rigorous data available on recidivism rates for given types of offenders released from different types of institution.[1]

Another widely accepted postulate is that rehabilitation varies directly with the frequency and intensity of communication between deviants and conforming persons, and inversely with communication among deviants. This is deducible from Sutherland's (1970: 75–77) differential association theory, which assumes that criminality is mainly the product of social learning in primary groups. Correctional institutions place deviants in close contact with other deviants, facilitating their social support of each other in rationalizing offenses. While they also bring deviants into contact with staff, the average ratio of staff to inmates in state and federal prisons is one to four (National Council on Crime and Delinquency, 1967: 192–197), a ratio that may mean only one staff member on duty to eight or more inmates on the main work shift, and to even more inmates at other times. This, plus the differences in class background and role between inmates and staff, impedes the prospect that staff communications to inmates

[1] A major problem in trying to determine relationships between recidivism rates and type of institution is that inmates with presumably the worst rates are sent to the most custodially oriented facilities and those presumed least criminal are sent to unwalled institutions. Therefore, one does not know whether difference in post-release behavior of inmates of the two types of edifices are due to differences in their construction or management or to differences in the character of the offenders they receive. By comparing only inmates with similar traits in open and closed British youth correctional facilities (called Borstals in England), Leslie T. Wilkins at first concluded that the open institutions reduced recidivism rates by about 10 percent. He then found, however, that this difference could be accounted for by what might be called a group norm effect that he noted in several studies: inmates of a given recidivism probability according to tabulation of prior experience with inmates of their type, who are confined with others of lower recidivism risk than themselves, had lower recidivism rates than predicted; those confined with worse risks than their own group had higher recidivism rates than predicted (Wilkins, 1965: 95–97). See also Beverly (1965) and Molof (1967) for California youth correction studies whose findings also appear to be explainable by a group norm effect.

can compete with communication among prisoners in affecting the thinking of individual inmates.

In traditional custodially oriented prisons, three categories of staff differ considerably in their communication with the prisoners. Custodial personnel are most numerous, and are also in most of the positions having highest authority. They stress social distance from inmates, barring any fraternization or familiarity. Treatment staff, especially psychologists and sociologists or social workers, but also chaplains and teachers, often strive for close communication, but are too few in number to achieve this with many inmates. The work supervision specialists—for example, the cooks, laundry managers, maintenance tradesmen, and factory foremen—are intermediate between custodial and treatment specialists in numbers and orientation towards inmates. They work in close and continuous interaction with inmates, often in a highly cooperative relationship as all try to complete a common task. Interviews with ex-prisoners who had clearly abandoned crime after considerable involvement in it, indicated that about half ascribed this anticriminal change to their prison experience, about half of these credited a staff member as most influential in their change, and about half of the prison personnel credited were work supervisors (Glaser, 1969: 90–94).

In many presumably progressive correctional institutions, effort is made to minimize differences between staff components and to maximize communication of all with prisoners. This was derived from the therapeutic community and milieu therapy ideals in institutions for the mentally ill, which recognized that all staff may have a rehabilitative influence on some patients. These facilities are characterized by the involvement of lowest with highest status staff in consultations on individual cases, by group counselling sessions in which all sources of tension among inmates and staff may be openly discussed, and by relative permissiveness and flexibility in discipline when dealing with deviance by inmates within the institution. Since prevention of escapes or disorder still are important to job security of staff, some role tension and ambiguity affects staff of such institutions when they are confronted with disciplinary problems (Cressey, 1965). Nevertheless, comparative studies of institutions with diverse inmate-staff relationships indicate that: (1) inmate-inmate communication varies directly with inmate-staff communication; (2) where social distance of staff from inmates is greatest, inmates most strongly emphasize a code of "doing your own time"—not trusting or helping other inmates, and develop a "rat complex"—quasi-paranoid hate and suspicion of other inmates as alleged informers to staff ("stool pigeons" or "rats"); (3) criminalistic and antistaff values characterize inmate leaders inversely with the extent of inmate-staff communication (Street *et al.,* 1966; Glaser, 1969: 61–73, 81–90; Grusky, 1959).

Correctional institutions that promote communication are presumed by their leaders to be more rehabilitative than traditional ones, but such follow-up data as we have suggests that the correlation of staff-inmate communication in formal group counselling programs with postrelease noncriminality is close to zero. This may well be because these programs are used (and appear to be effective) primarily as a management device, to reduce inmate-staff tensions by permitting the ready airing and resolution of grievances (Harrison and Mueller, 1964; Seckel, 1965). However, there are indications from other research that a near zero relationship of special counselling programs to recidivism is due to countervailing relationships: communication promotion reduces recidivism rates for inmates with low previous criminality who are articulate, but increases it for those with most extensive prior criminality (Adams, 1970; Carney, 1969; Grant and Grant, 1959). The latter apparently exploit rather than internalize the permissive counselling oriented relationships but are deterred somewhat by traditional methods of prison operation.

Analysis of the effectiveness of mental hospitals in changing the behavior of the mentally ill poses some problems even more difficult than those indicated for correctional institutions. This is partly due to the differences between the inmates of the two types of institution, and partly due to the different grounds and procedure for their confinement. Mental illness is ascribed to a person on the basis of a wide variety of rather ambiguous symptoms, including almost any deviance people find puzzling, but particularly, deviations from the presumed "normal" in the extent of social withdrawal, fantasy, emotional variability, situational irrelevance of emotions or acts, unrealistic accusations, and unrealistic self-depictions. Because of this diversity, Thomas Scheff (1966) has appropriately called mental illness "residual deviance." There is considerable disagreement over his further contention that these ailments may be primarily secondary deviance, due to the consequences of being labelled mentally ill.

Scheff (1966: 92ff.) points out that in the procedure required for a court order committing people to mental hospitals, interviews by court psychiatrists are often perfunctory, yet the psychiatrists usually endorse the petition to the court that the person be adjudged "insane" and be committed. He points out further that hospital staff assume all patients must be ill, and insist that a first step to recovery must be the patients' recognition of their illness. Therefore, social rewards in the hospital and prospects for release are contingent on the patient seeing himself as ill. Scheff's contention is that labelling and psychiatric treatment result in such influences on the patient to see himself as mentally ill, that he adjusts by manifesting mental illness symptoms; in Scheff's view, having a "career" of mental illness is due primarily to being labelled by others as mentally ill.

In criticism of Scheff's theory it can be pointed out that both court decisions and psychiatric recommendations on involuntary commitment to a mental hospital usually are not based on any single interview. Instead, the psychiatrist and the court receive and accept first-, second-, or third-hand accounts of observations by family members, police, teachers, employers, or others. These report seeing the person in question repeatedly manifest some combination of symptoms of mental illness. Indeed, family members usually long resist seeing the patient as mentally ill and try to ignore repeated incidents and reports of aberrant behavior (Sampson *et al.,* 1962; Hollingshead and Redlich, 1958: Chapter 6). In the commitment decisions the reported behavioral history is stressed more than one interview for the court because symptoms are not expected to be uniform and continuous. The decision to try to have the person committed usually comes only after the cited behavioral history is followed by precipitating events involving one or more of the following: (1) the person manifests a new extreme of his symptoms in a form that involves serious danger to himself or others; (2) he ceases to work, to clean himself, or even to feed himself; (3) people at home who tolerated and compensated for these or less drastic symptoms no longer are available (for example, a spouse leaves, the indulgent mother dies, or caretakers become "fed up") (Sampson, *et al.*, 1962).

It should also be pointed out with respect to the labelling theory that many persons themselves seek care for mental illness—including hospitalization—when they are the ones most concerned about their continued emotional instability, fears, inability to concentrate, or other symptoms. These, however, are the patients for whom prognoses are most favorable and release occurs earliest (Denzin and Spitzer, 1968). Furthermore, research on the effects of drugs in inducing or terminating moods and hallucinations is providing increasing evidence that for many—perhaps most—mental illness careers there is a persistent organic primary source, apart from labelling (despite the possibility that organic conditions sometimes produce mental illness symptoms only indirectly, by creating sensations a subject interprets as evidence of mental illness, and so labels himself as insane).[2] In addition, psychologists pioneering in behavior modification, notably Teodoro Ayllon and Nathan Azrin (1968) and Gerald R. Patterson (1967), have shown that many mental illness symptoms—even a catatonic's extreme helplessness and immobility for a decade or longer—are responses to subtle rewards the subject receives from others for this behavior, and can be modified by altering the rewards. These rewarding reactions of others to the symptoms usually start in the family, and precede—rather than involve—labelling.

While such criticisms suffice to prevent secondary deviance from fully replacing other explanations of mental illness, they do not warrant complete dismissal of Scheff's critique. Once a person is tagged mentally ill by someone, those who accept the label as valid often review the life history of the person in a biased way,

---

[2] There is increasing evidence that many chronic mental illness symptoms result from abnormalities in the body's production or use of cathecolamines. These are a group of related chemicals, and include the hormones adrenaline and noradrenaline. They affect the regulation of moods and the body's utilization of other hormones, as well as production of norepinephrine, which is involved in transmission of nerve impulses and varies in the brain with fluctuations of emotion (Fieve, 1970). Organically produced sensations, however, may sometimes induce labels of mental illness only by being perceived as symptoms (Becker, 1967).

to justify the label to themselves or others—even to the one so categorized. Accounts of past events may thereby be distorted, either deliberately or unwittingly. Lawyers have pointed out that in traditional commitment procedures there is a great possibility and occasional occurrence of involuntary hospitalization on the basis of unwarranted gossip, prejudice, personal vindictiveness, or selfish interest in having someone removed from the community. This resulted in laws in California in 1969, and elsewhere recently, requiring definite proof that the person is a danger to himself or others—rather than merely distasteful to someone—before he can be involuntarily hospitalized.

Labelling is in other ways an important part of both causation and rehabilitation for many types of deviance. Much—perhaps most—effort to change deviants necessarily consists of an effort to get them to strive for new self-labels. From the standpoint of the dominant element in society, a change in the reference group and hence in the preferred self-label is the prime rehabilitative objective when dealing with deviants who have a stake in nonconformity because their reference group is deviant. This is especially evident in efforts to change those with deviant beliefs or tastes, such as those whose beliefs run to atheism or whose tastes run to homosexuality or to a "hippie" life style.

Mental institution confinement has been shortened or eliminated entirely in recent years by use of tranquilizers and other chemotherapy, as well as by the growth of community mental health treatment facilities for outpatients. Meanwhile, education and vocational training, as contributions to the rehabilitation of all types of deviant, have been made more effective by such innovations as programmed learning, "token economy" systems of immediate rewards for learning (Ulman and Krasner, 1965; Ayllon and Azrin, 1968), and sheltered workshops in the community for employment of the mentally retarded or disturbed or the physically handicapped (Raush and Raush, 1968), as well as by subsidizing employers who hire and train stigmatized persons. As a result of these and other trends to be described in the next subsection, the population of U.S. mental hospitals declined from a peak of 560,000 in 1950 to an estimated 400,000 in 1970, and the number of inmates in state and federal prisons declined from a peak of 220,000 in 1961 to 195,000 in 1967, despite population increases in these periods. The total days in mental hospitals per 1,000 U.S. population declined from 1,720 in 1945 to 1,060 in 1968. Staff per 100 patients rose from 24 in 1950 to 55 in 1968, while cost per patient per day increased from $2.43 in 1950 to $11.25 in 1968 (Bureau of the Census, 1970). Staff and cost changes may largely account for the shorter stays.

REINTEGRATION

The ultimate test of rehabilitation is conformity in the community, rather than in an institution. For this reason, much rehabilitation effort is undertaken without—or after—institutionalization. In all such activity it is clear that changing the deviant is not always sufficient for social control; one must also achieve his acceptance by conforming society, and what is sometimes independent of this, his perception of himself as either currently or eventually accepted.

Emergent trends in mental hospitals and prisons reflect increased tempering of restraint not only by efforts at rehabilitation, but also by concern with reintegration. Instead of separating patients by ailment or prognosis, they are now grouped within many state hospitals by the metropolitan neighborhood or the town in which they reside, and visiting by relatives is encouraged, to preserve home ties.

One alternative to imprisonment began in the United States in 1867 when Massachusetts passed the first probation law. Probation is a court's requirement that an offender undergo a period of supervision in the community, usually without initial imprisonment. If the probationer seriously misbehaves in this period, probation may be replaced by a prison sentence. As was noted earlier, this has been especially successful with first offenders having a high "stake in conformity."

The term "parole" was initiated early in the history of the Elmira Reformatory to designate a procedure whereby correctional administrators release prisoners before their term of sentence is over, but may reimprison them for failure to abide by stipulated rules when in the community. Similar procedures, called ticket of leave, were developed earlier in Australia and Ireland. Parole and probation administrators require that the offenders they supervise seek and maintain legitimate employment, avoid criminal associates, refrain from excessive drink or other deviance, and report regularly to the parole or probation officer. All of these requirements are presumed to foster integration in nondeviant society.

In 1899 in Chicago the first juvenile court was established and such courts spread rapidly throughout the United States and the rest of the world. They brought to the adjudication of juveniles a much less formal procedure than that of courts for adults. In addition, they were concerned not just with crime by juveniles, but also with a wide range of behavior presumed to be conducive to crime, such as impudence to parents or teachers and truancy from home or school. This was done on the basis of argument that the state should exercise a protective role, in behalf of the child, whenever the parents were found incapable or unwilling to rear the child properly. It has been charged, however, that the major motivation for the juvenile court was middle class abhorrence of the behavior of lower class youth, and prejudice by the politically dominant descendants of older immigrants to the United States, from northern and western Europe, against the customs of the more recent and poorer immigrants, from southern and eastern Europe (Platt, 1969).

It has also been charged that the informal procedures of juvenile courts and their hasty activity (due to their excessive caseloads), lead to judges' callously committing youth to correctional institutions on the basis of inadequate evidence of the alleged misbehavior. In 1967 a Supreme Court decision (*in re Gault*) required more definite charges and more formal procedures in juvenile courts. Its impact was much less drastic than a literal interpretation of its wording might have led one to expect, for juvenile court staff were reluctant to change the procedures with which they were accustomed, as these require less time and effort than more formal processes. In any event, only about half the juveniles taken into custody by the police are referred to the courts, although this proportion varies greatly from city to city. Informal processing, whether by the police or the courts, permits prejudices to influence decisions more than is usual in formal procedure, and prejudices are self-validating if officials assume a juvenile is delinquent on the basis of his class, ethnicity, or other attribute instead of examining the evidence carefully and objectively. Informal procedures, however, facilitate mediation of conflicts between the juvenile and others, make counseling easier, and minimize social stigmatization by the trial process.

Parole, probation, and the analogous conditional release procedures known as aftercare in mental hospitals and some other institutions for deviants are all justified by their proponents as facilitating reintegration into conforming society. In practice, however, most of these measures provide only brief and infrequent staff-client contacts; the releasee merely reports to his supervisor's office, often for only a perfunctory interview, and this occurs but once per week or even once per month. This permits neither assistance nor surveillance to have an appreciable impact on the client's employment, leisure time associates, recreational activity, or other presumed prerequisites of conventional life. Staff influence on clients can be much greater when there is daily contact between them over many hours, as in the rapidly growing practices of initial release of the client in the daytime hours only, for employment or education outside the treatment residence.

In "work release" programs at jails, prisons and mental hospitals, reentry into the community to hold a job or attend school occurs on a daily basis before the client's freedom is extended to permit more participation in community recreational activity and ultimately, he is allowed to reside in the community. Thus transition from the role of inmate to the roles of a free citizen can be graduated, with assistance at each stage in which difficulties occur, as well as surveillance, to assure conformity in one conventional role before freedom is extended to other roles.

Because confinement institutions usually are located in rural areas or small towns, but most of their inmates are from metropolitan areas, graduated release also is accomplished in special correctional or mental health halfway house or community treatment residences in metropolitan areas. Institution inmates are transferred there a few months prior to their expected date of complete release. Sometimes such centers are used in place of regular institutional confinement—for example, as a temporary home for probationers—so that they represent a placement "halfway in" rather than "out" of a traditional institution. In some cases also, instead of being residences from which occupants go forth daily for work

or recreation, they are centers for intensive counselling and training, or sheltered workplaces, to which the clients come daily while
residing at home.

Work and education releases on a daily basis, and halfway
houses, permit both counselling and diagnosis to focus on the
subjects' immediate problems outside the institution, instead of
only on their behavior in the artificial setting of the institution,
or on the untestable accounts of a more distant past institution
residents construct to rationalize their current status. The prime
danger with halfway houses and sheltered workhouses is that they
sometimes become over-regimented, with staff oriented more to ad-
justing the clients to life in these facilities than to preparing them
for an autonomous life in the free community (Scott, 1969).

In the 1950s there began over a decade of controlled experiments in reduction of caseloads for probation and parole officers.
These yielded no sustained differences, especially on probation,
or resulted in somewhat less recidivism in experimental than in
control groups only for those offenders who were classified in
medium risk categories; the best risk cases had low recidivism
rates and the poorest risk categories had high rates regardless of
the size caseload they were in (Adams, 1967). Low impact of
reduced caseloads on probation appears to reflect the fact that
higher priorities and rewards are given to presentence reporting
than to supervision or assistance in probation offices (Glaser,
1969).

Later experiments of intensive intervention have stressed
different styles of community supervision for different psychological and cultural types of delinquent, with caseloads of only
10 to 12 as compared to parole caseloads of 70 per officer. Essentially, a fair but firm approach is stressed for criminally en-
culturated or manipulative delinquents, more supportive and therapeutic orientations are used for psychologically immature or neu-
rotic delinquents, while all who seem to need it receive tutoring,
family counseling, and other special services. Those assigned to the
pioneer community treatment programs were randomly selected
from California Youth Authority communities in the Sacramento-
Stockton area, with those not selected forming a control group
that were in the regular state training schools an average of eight
months before parole. While the parole cases had distinctly higher

recidivism and parole violation rates, there is some contention that this is because there was less reporting of infractions in the community treatment cases (Gibbons, 1970). Conversely, those in the program claim that intensive supervision of the community treatment cases made for more staff awareness of and action on infractions than occurs on parole. They also point to the distinctly superior record of the community treatment cases for whom the match between style of supervision and type of delinquent was that prescribed as optimum (Warren, 1968, 1970).

Perhaps the most promising type of intensive intervention programs team each probation or parole officer with one or more persons indigenous to the neighborhood of his clients, and of the same background, or even an ex-offender. These "community treatment specialists" or "probation aides" are often expected to work primarily on evenings and weekends. Operating as teams, one or another is available at any time to supply instant and very personal aid for the persons assigned to their supervision, and for the families of these persons. This aid varies from mediating quarrels to helping in child care and housecleaning during emergencies, and to facilitating procurement of employment or of social welfare service for their clientele (Cocks, 1968; Glaser, 1971: 38–39).

It may be difficult to achieve the staff-client trust and cooperation needed for rehabilitation and reintegration of a deviant when the state's concern with him begins in actions officially designated as punishment or revenge-seeking, and implying rejection. These connotations are not avoided by the juvenile court's informal procedures and its separation from the adult court, for they still involve the police and correctional confinement operations analogous to those traditional for adult criminals. More recently there has been an effort to avoid this by what Jesse R. Pitts has called the medicalization of deviance. This is illustrated in the replacement of jails and prisons by medical aid centers, civil commitment institutions, and after-care centers for persons found delinquent, alcoholic, drug addicted, or sexually deviant or found not guilty of felonies on grounds of insanity. Pitts (1968) points out that advantages of medicalization for social control include: (1) greater immunity of staff from corruption and political pressure than prevails in law enforcement or judicial agencies; (2) less ready rationalization by the deviant that he is unjustifiably defined as much more evil than others, for he is treated as sick rather than bad; (3) greater flexibility in treatment, including more receptivity to controlled experimentation and other research; and (4) a less permanent stigmatization of the deviant, since he can ultimately be designated as recuperated.

Despite these ostensible advantages, medicalized social control agencies are often impeded because: (1) their initial intake still occurs through traditional police and court procedures, with stigmatization, corruption, and long confinement in jail a frequent prospect before coming to the medicalized agency; (2) with those deviants prone to predation, such as delinquents or civilly-committed drug addicts, the medicalized agencies are sometimes as much concerned with restraint as are traditional correctional institutions, and such concern impedes reintegration efforts; (3) as large organizations, they often have callous and impersonal bureaucratic staff; (4) the shortage of professional staff and the caste-like barriers between them and other staff reduce the effectiveness of treatment services; and (5) social class and other differences in background and frame of reference impede rapport between all staff and most of the deviants they treat.

Because ex-deviants have been accepted in both deviant and conforming society, they bridge the two, and are thereby uniquely qualified to aid in the reintegration of deviants. Alcoholics Anonymous was the pioneer organization of such persons preoccupied with helping those in what was previously their own deviant condition. An offshoot for drug addicts, Synanon, has splintered and resplintered into scores of similarly functioning ex-addict organizations (Daytop Village, Reality House, Phoenix Houses and dozens of others in the New York City area; Gateway House in Chicago; The Family in San Francisco). Recovery, Inc. for ex-mental hospital patients and the Fortune Society for ex-convicts perform analogous functions (Sagarin, 1969). Many of these groups now accept diverse types of deviant.

The primary tenets of these ex-deviant groups always include at least two elements: (1) a derogatory view of their deviant condition (e.g. as immoral, stupid or a biological weakness); (2) a belief that they can keep from resuming deviance only by helping others to become ex-deviant. These usually are supplemented by other principles, such as a commitment to complete honesty with each other, but all of these beliefs and their implementations serve one purpose: to shift their identification of themselves from deviant to conforming. By persuading others to change, they increase their own commitment to change. In addition, operating in small cohesive groups they give each other interpersonal warmth, aid, and obligation, thereby replacing attractions of this sort that they may previously have found in deviant groups.

From the standpoint of a dominant group seeking complete social control of deviants, these ex-deviant organizations have advantages and limitations. It is now widely accepted that their members have a unique rapport with deviants because they have had the same experiences, yet exemplify the feasibility of transition to nondeviant status; this makes them very effective as what Lofland (1969: 212–220) calls normal-smiths—people who effectively communicate to the deviants a perception of them as normal human beings. For this reason ex-deviant organizations are often subsidized by the state and are sometimes installed in prisons and mental hospitals; civil service positions have been created specifying ex-deviant status as a qualification rather than a barrier (for example, ex-addict Narcotic Rehabilitation Aides in the New York State Narcotic Addiction Control Commission). Three limitations make them less than a panacea for deviance, however.

First, like other sources of voluntary treatment, ex-deviant organizations only reach persons suffering extreme stress from their deviance—people who have hit bottom, as Alcoholics Anonymous puts it. When a person is adjusted to his deviance and finds it attractive, he resists efforts to change him. That is why even the most effective of these organizations only acquires in its ranks a minority of the deviants it tries to recruit. That is also why social control is only achieved by restraint for some deviants. Treatment efforts appear to be most effective for rehabilitation when voluntarily sought, but not necessarily ineffective when provided in combination with restraint (Brill and Lieberman, 1969).

Second, although for some types of deviance, notably alcohol and drug addiction, ex-deviant organizations may claim more successful social control than any other method that defines "success" as complete abstinence, the success is persistent for only a minority of the persons recruited. Unfortunately, these organizations do not keep and publish adequate follow-up statistics, but some follow-up of ex-addict groups is possible in New York where over a score of the leading organizations receive state funds, for which they must report all cases admitted and all terminated. A six-month unpublished state follow-up of those admitted by one organization in 1968 revealed that 80 percent had terminated in this period. To avoid this type of statistic, most of the organizations have a pre-admission ordeal, such as days or weeks of waiting, verbal abuse, and dirty work, to assure high motivation of those counted as members. When they publish follow-up statistics, they only include in their sample those who have been there some minimum number of months—or in one case, several years with "good behavior"—and they often have highly variable follow-up periods. It is readily apparent when one is in continual contact with them that many members "split" in moments of stress. A large proportion of the persons in public and private addiction treatment agencies, including ex-addict groups, now are persons previously in and out of the same or other groups and agencies. As already indicated, most addicts seem to experience cycles of abstinence and relapse, and the probability of subsequent abstinence does seem to be enhanced with each successive abstinence period.

Finally, even the successes are not always highly integrated in conventional society, a large proportion being abstinent only while resident in and socially and economically dependent upon the organization, which in turn survives primarily from public contributions. While this is a partial conformity to conventional life standards, it is far from complete conformity to them.

Talcott Parsons' (1951: 314–318) general paradigm of four stages for all social control of deviant behavior, which he applied particularly to the analysis of psychotherapy, seems to describe well the efforts of ex-deviants or any other "normal-smiths" in achieving the complete reintegration of an individual into a group which had rejected him as deviant. The first stage is *support:* the deviant is assured that he is not rejected by the normal-smith and that he is accepted as capable of conforming. It should be noted that ex-deviants do not have a monopoly of supportive ability, and indeed, some have a reaction-formation of hyperintolerance towards those whose deviance they once shared. This seems especially common among former adherents of deviant religious or political belief. Furthermore, some nondeviants are tested and found dependably supportive by deviants (for example, non-rejecting old friends or relatives, therapists, and priests long in close contact with the deviants). The second stage, although stages overlap, is *permissiveness:* the deviant is not held responsible for recurrences of his deviant behavior as long as he is trying. The third stage is *restriction of reciprocity:* while recurrence of deviance is accepted it is not supported, and thus the change agent is not drawn into the deviancy. This may arouse hostility in the deviant, but that is not reciprocated. In Parsons' terms, functional specificity and affective neutrality govern the normal-smith's role at this point. The fourth stage is providing *esteem,* that is, *rewarding* any conformity the deviant manifests.

In an elaboration of this paradigm, Parsons, Bales, and Shils (1953: 238–245) point out that institutionalization of the therapist's specialized and impersonal role permits him to restrict reciprocity, and to reward simply by pronouncing the client "much better" or "cured," without accepting the client into his own social group or forming a new "deviant subcollectivity" of therapists and ex-patients. In the case of the ex-addict organizations, the lack of institutionalized authority may make their only effective reward to the deviant his inclusion into a new primary group, the organization itself, which remains somewhat marginal to the real society, if not clearly deviant. This group's role relationships, in Parsons' pattern variable terminology, are functionally diffuse and affective, exactly the opposite of the professional's relationship to his client. It may well be, however, that this affective and diffuse reward capacity is exactly why the ex-addict groups are more successful as social control agents than professionals, at least for some deviants.

EVALUATION OF SOCIAL CONTROL EFFECTIVENESS

Advocates of all of the six "Rs," and of all variations in each, claim some effectiveness in fostering the ultimate reintegration of some deviants into conforming society. Each can point to the presumed "success" cases of his approach, but with every approach there are also some cases that apparently were unaffected or may have even had their deviance enhanced, and in most success cases the sources of change are somewhat debatable. There has been in-adequate measurement of impact for every method of social control. Perhaps the most important of many reasons for the paucity of precise knowledge are: (1) the division of responsibility for se-quential social control operations among largely autonomous and poorly coordinated agencies; (2) reluctance to experiment with social control methods; and (3) difficulties in obtaining adequate data on the long-run careers of deviants dealt with by various methods.

The police are involved in the initial stages of efforts at con-trol for almost every type of deviant, from predator to prostitute and from drunk to schizophrenic. They are the only agency on call twenty-four hours per day and seven days per week to aid in coping with almost every type of crisis in human behavior. Police handling of each case on any particular occasion generally is for a short period only. They either transfer the persons they deem require longer social control to courts or other agencies or they release them. Their decision to question or to detain, however, and their interaction with the detainee, may vary from harassment to assist-ance and may have diverse consequences in fostering or reducing further deviance in different types of persons or circumstances. Police measure their effectiveness as a percentage of complaints cleared by arrest or determined to be unfounded, rather than as a percentage of cases altered effectively by police action or by the agencies to which the police transferred them.

Among the many important reasons for this lack of an ade-quate measure of the effectiveness of social control policies is the fact that the police are usually in the executive branch of municipal government (and highly independent even within that branch), courts form the judicial component of government and most often operate on a county basis, while the treatment agencies to which they commit deviants are operated by the executive branch, and most of the larger institutions are under state government. None of these several agencies must report systematically to the others in this social control sequence, and so each cannot regularly know what consequences its actions may have had on the subsequent behavior of the deviants it handled.

Correctional and mental health agencies deal with each deviant for a longer period than do police or courts, as a rule, so they can more directly assess their effectiveness in altering the behavior of deviants. However, many inmates are discharged from institutions with little or no parole or aftercare, and for the others this postrelease supervision is administered independently of the institutions. Therefore, the information of institution officials on their effectiveness is largely in terms of the adjustment of deviants to institutional life, rather than in terms of their postrelease conduct in the community. Furthermore, in this atomized administrative structure, only the institutional adjustment of the deviants affects immediately and appreciably the satisfactions or difficulties experienced by an institution official.

Even the small percentage of police, courts, or correctional or mental health agencies that do collect systematic information on the subsequent behavior of the deviants they handle cannot readily know the impact of their practices on this behavior. There are two reasons for this lack of knowledge. First, subsequent behavior may be more a function of the types of deviant involved and the social settings to which they are released than of the manner in which the agency handled them. Second, in most cases several different agencies and components of agencies deal with a deviant between the initiation and termination of social control efforts, and it is difficult to differentiate the separate impacts of each.

Despite these problems, statistical assessment of social control practices is possible if one can compare the postrelease behavior of large groups of deviants that differ only in the manner in which they were handled at one stage in their processing as deviants. This comparison is accomplished ideally by controlled experiments, as when all deviants at one stage are randomly assigned to alternative subsequent programs.

Public concern that an equal amount of restraint be imposed on all similar deviants, or that every case receive what is postulated to be optimum treatment, has traditionally impeded much random assignment of cases to different treatments to measure which is most effective. Nevertheless, some deliberate experiments have been conducted in recent years, usually through reducing restraint in conjunction with providing a new mode of treatment initially to a randomly selected fraction of all those who might have received it. In addition, much quasi-experimentation has occurred unwittingly through sudden changes in treatment practice, thus permitting "before" and "after" measurements. Also, assignment of cases to diverse programs by courts and administrators has often been so haphazard that researchers have been able to compare groups of ostensibly similar deviants assigned to different programs. Even in these instances postrelease information is often difficult to procure on the subjects studied, as official records are poor or inaccessible to researchers (Glaser, 1965, 1971; Wilkins, 1969). A rational social control organization would allocate several percentage points of its budget to systematic evaluation, but the total expended on research currently is only a fraction of one per cent of the social control budget.

REFERENCES

Adams, Stuart
  1967   "Some findings from correctional caseload research." Federal Probation 31 (December): 48–57.
  1970   "The PICO Project," in Norman Johnston, Leonard Savitz and Marvin E. Wolfgang (eds.), The Sociology of Punishment and Correction, 2d ed. New York: Wiley.
Ayllon, Teodoro, and Nathan Azrin
  1968   The Token Economy. New York: Appleton-Century-Crofts.
Becker, Howard S.
  1967   "History, culture and subjective experience: an exploration of the social bases of drug-induced experiences," Journal of Health and Social Behavior 8 (September): 163–176.
Beverly, Robert F.
  1965   An Analysis of Parole Performance by Institution of Release. Research Report No. 40. Sacramento, Calif.: Division of the Youth Authority.
Brill, Leon, and Louis Lieberman
  1969   Authority and Addiction. Boston: Little, Brown.
Bureau of the Census, U.S. Department of Commerce
  1970   Statistical Abstract of the United States—1970. Washington: U.S. Government Printing Office.

Carney, Francis J.
  1969 "Correctional research and correctional decision-making: some problems and prospects," Journal of Research on Crime and Delinquency 6 (July): 110–122.
Chambliss, William J.
  1967 "Types of deviance and the effectiveness of legal sanctions." Wisconsin Law Review 1967 (Summer): 703–719.
Cocks, Jack
  1968 "From 'WHISP' to 'RODEO'." California Youth Authority Quarterly 21 (Winter): 7–11.
Cressey, Donald R.
  1965 "Prison organizations." In James G. March (ed.), Handbook of Organizations. Chicago: Rand McNally.
Denzin, Norman K., and Stephen P. Spitzer
  1968 "Paths to the mental hospital and staff predictions of patient role behavior." In Spitzer and Denzin (eds.), The Mental Patient. New York: McGraw-Hill.
Durkheim, Emile
  1947 The Division of Labor in Society. George Simpson, transl. New York: Free Press.
Fieve, Donald R.
  1970 "Interdisciplinary studies of manic-depressive psychosis." In Mental Health Program Reports, No. 4, National Clearing House for Mental Health Information, Publication 5026. Washington: U.S. Government Printing Office.
Garfinkel, Harold
  1956 "Conditions of successful degradation ceremonies." American Journal of Sociology 61 (March): 420–424.
Glaser, Daniel
  1965 "Correctional research: an elusive paradise." Journal of Research on Crime and Delinquency 2 (January): 1–11.
  1969 "Research on probation." In Alvin W. Cohn (ed.), Problems, Thoughts and Processes in Criminal Justice Administration. New York: National Council on Crime and Delinquency.
  1970a "Violence and the city." In Glaser (ed.), Crime in the City. New York: Harper & Row.

1970b   "Some notes on urban jails." In Glaser (ed.), Crime in
         the City. New York: Harper & Row.
1971   "Five practical research suggestions for correctional ad-
         ministrators." Crime and Delinquency 17 (January):
         32–40.
Glaser, Daniel, and Vincent O'Leary
1966   Personal Characteristics and Parole Outcome. Washing-
         ton: U.S. Government Printing Office.
Grant, Douglas, and Marguerite Q. Grant
1959   "A group dynamics approach to the treatment of non-
         conformists in the Navy," Annals of the American
         Academy of Political and Social Science 323 (March):
         126–135.
Gibbons, Don C.
1970   "Differential treatment of delinquents and interpersonal
         maturity levels theory: a critique." Social Service Review
         44 (March): 22–33.
Grusky, Oscar
1959   "Organizational goals and the behavior of informal lead-
         ers." American Journal of Sociology 65 (July): 59–67.
Harrison, Robert M., and Paul F. C. Mueller
1964   Clue-Hunting About Group Counseling and Parole Out-
         come. Sacramento, Calif.: Dept. of Corrections, Re-
         search Report No. 11.
Hollingshead, August B., and Frederick R. Redlich
1958   Social Class and Mental Illness. New York: Wiley.
Jacks, Harold
1967   A 20-Year Study of Convicted Parole Violators. Harris-
         burg: Pennsylvania Board of Parole.
LaPiere, Richard T.
1934   "Attitudes vs. action," Social Forces 13 (December):
         230–237.
Linsky, Arnold S.
1970   "Community homogeneity and exclusion of the mentally
         ill: rejection vs. consensus about deviance." Journal of
         Health and Social Behavior 11 (December): 304–311.
Lofland, John
1969   Deviance and Identity. Englewood Cliffs, N.J.: Prentice-
         Hall.

Molof, Martin J.
   1967   Forestry Camp Study. Sacramento, Calif.: Division of
           the Youth Authority, Research Report No. 53.
National Council on Crime and Delinquency
   1967   "Correction in the United States." Crime and Delin-
           quency 13 (January): 142–145. (Also published as
           Appendix A to President's Commission on Law Enforce-
           ment and the Administration of Justice, Task Force Re-
           port: Corrections. Washington: U.S. Government Print-
           ing Office, 1967).
Newton, George D., and Franklin E. Zimring
   1969   Firearms and Violence in American Life. Staff Report
           No. 7, National Commission on the Causes and Preven-
           tion of Violence. Washington: U.S. Government Printing
           Office.
Parsons, Talcott
   1951   The Social System. New York: Free Press.
Parsons, Talcott, Robert F. Bales and Edward A. Shils
   1953   Working Papers in the Theory of Action. New York:
           Free Press.
Parsons, Talcott, and Winston White
   1961   "The link between character and society." In Seymour
           M. Lipset and Leo Lowenthal (eds.), Culture and Social
           Character. New York: Free Press.
Patterson, Gerald R., and Beverly Fagot
   1967   "Selective responsiveness to social reinforcers and deviant
           behavior in children." Psychological Record 17 (July):
           369–378.
Phillipson, Coleman
   1923   Three Criminal Law Reformers: Beccaria, Bentham,
           Romilly. London: Dent.
Pitts, Jesse R.
   1968   "Social control: (1) the concept." In International En-
           cyclopedia of the Social Sciences. New York: Macmillan,
           Free Press.
Platt, Anthony
   1969   The Child Savers: The Invention of Delinquency. Chi-
           cago: University of Chicago Press.

Raush, Harold L., and Charlotte L. Raush
  1968 The Halfway House Movement. New York: Appleton-Century-Crofts.
Ross, H. Laurence, Donald T. Campbell and Gene V. Glass
  1970 "Determining the social effects of a legal reform: the British 'Breathalyzer' Crackdown of 1967." American Behavioral Scientist 13 (March/April): 493–509.
Sagarin, Edward
  1969 Odd Man In. Chicago: Quadrangle.
Sampson, Harold, Sheldon L. Messinger and Robert O. Towne
  1962 "Family processes and becoming a mental patient." American Journal of Sociology 68 (July): 88–96.
Scheff, Thomas J.
  1966 Being Mentally Ill. Chicago: Aldine.
Schwartz, Richard D., and Jerome N. Skolnick
  1962 "Two studies of legal stigma." Social Problems 10 (Fall): 133–142.
Scott, Robert A.
  1969 The Making of Blind Men: A Study of Adult Socialization. New York: Russell Sage Foundation.
Seckel, Joachim P.
  1965 Experiments in Group Counseling at Two Youth Authority Institutions. Sacramento, Calif.: Division of the Youth Authority, Research Report No. 46.
Street, David, Robert D. Vinter and Charles Perrow
  1966 Organization for Treatment. New York: Free Press.
Sutherland, Edwin H., and Donald R. Cressey
  1970 Criminology. 8th ed. Philadelphia: Lippincott.
Tittle, Charles R.
  1969 "Crime rates and legal sanctions." Social Problems 16 (Spring): 409–423.
Toernudd, Patrick
  1968 "The preventive effect of fines for drunkenness." Scandinavian Studies in Criminology, Vol. 2. Oslo: Universitetsforlaget.
Ulman, L. P., and L. Krasner, eds.
  1965 Case Studies in Behavior Modification. New York: Holt, Rinehart & Winston.

Wahl, Albert, and Daniel Glaser
  1963   "A pilot time study of the federal probation officer's job." Federal Probation 27 (September): 20–24.
Walker, Nigel
  1965   Crime and Punishment in Britain. Edinburgh: University Press.
Warner, Lyle G., and Melvin L. DeFleur
  1969   "Attitude as an interactional concept: social constraint and social distance as intervening variables between attitudes and action." American Sociological Review 34 (April): 153–169.
Warren, Marguerite Q.
  1968   The Community Treatment Project After Five Years. Sacramento, Calif.: Department of the Youth Authority.
  1970   The Case for Differential Treatment of Delinquents. Sacramento, Calif.: Institute for the Study of Crime and Delinquency.
Wilkins, Leslie T.
  1965   Social Deviance. Englewood Cliffs, N.J.: Prentice-Hall.
  1969   Evaluation of Penal Measures. New York: Random House.
Williams, Robin M.
  1964   Strangers Next Door. Englewood Cliffs, N.J.: Prentice-Hall.
Wolfgang, Marvin E., and Franco Ferracuti
  1967   The Subculture of Violence. New York: Barnes and Noble.
Zeisel, Hans
  1969   "Methodological problems in studies of sentencing." Law and Society Review 3 (May): 621–631.

6
THE DYNAMICS OF DEFINING DEVIANCE

Perfect social control of deviance is achieved without any of the methods discussed in the preceding chapter, and with no action by the deviant, whenever society's definitions change so as to make acceptable that which it once rejected. Redefinition of this sort has occurred repeatedly with regard to deviant beliefs, consumption, selling, performance, and status, although not appreciably with in-group predation or suicide.

The historical phenomena of deviance redefinition raise theoretical questions: How does an act come to be defined as deviant in a society? What fosters change in this definition? Is there a fixed amount of behavior or status defined as deviant in the United States, so that anything no longer regarded as deviant is replaced by calling something else deviant? Is there a general trend of increase or decrease in the proportion of the population regarded as deviant?

The term "moral entrepreneur" was coined by Howard S. Becker (1963: Chapter 8) to designate anyone who promotes in a society the idea that something is deviant. Such a person endeavors to gain support for his ideas on what people should or should not do, and sometimes becomes part of a social movement in their behalf. Most of this entrepreneurial effort is directed at the state, calling for additions to the criminal law to extend the range of deviance for which courts may impose penalties. Such efforts resulted in the Prohibition Amendment, as well as in laws against opiate and marijuana possession, public gambling, pornography, "indecent exposure," and many other types of deviance (see Quinney, 1970: 65–97, for several examples).

One important observation that should be made on moral entrepreneurship, however, is that the laws against predation have a history quite different from that of the laws against deviant consumption, selling, performance, belief, or status. The definition of predation as deviant has been crescive, while the definition of other acts and statuses as deviance has been episodic. Because ingroup predations create clear-cut victims and threaten the security of person or property, popular sympathies aroused by them vary more in intensity than in direction. Rarely if ever do people try to repeal a law against predation; they only try to alter the penalties or the definitions. Insurance companies and others with special interests, rather than the types of persons or movements usually regarded as moral entrepreneurs, have been the main promoters of new definitions or sanctions for predation, particularly on property offenses (see, for example, Schroeder, 1950).

For deviance other than predation, the moral entrepreneur frequently must persuade others to define as criminal that which they at first perceived only as atypical. Acts or statuses that do not victimize anyone are not as clearly threatening as predation. The task of the moral entrepreneur is to portray them as threatening. This usually involves three rather standard contentions: (1) the deviant injures himself, either in this world or in an afterlife; (2) the deviance is contagious (if not eliminated it will spread to our children or even to us); (3) the deviance, though not predatory in itself, is conducive to predation, and is thereby threatening.

These three themes have been repeated over and over again, with innumerable variations, for every type of deviance except predation. Temperance leaders described "Demon Rum" as making the drinker slothful, the drinker as enticing the innocent to share his vice, and the drunkard as molesting women and stealing from his friends and family. Marijuana and opiate users were described as destroying their own sanity, "pushing" their habit among school children, and committing heinous crimes while crazed by drugs. All ethnic minorities against whom there has been prejudice by the white Anglo-Saxon Protestant (WASP) dominant group have been described as morally depraved, as lusting for WASP females or children, and as unfair competitors of WASPs in economic pursuits.

In moral entrepreneurial activities, arguments usually are exaggerated. The charges are so extreme that compromise would seem illogical. Laws against deviance therefore often begin by creating an utter metamorphosis in state policy, changing complete permissiveness to absolute prohibition or exclusion. This was evident in our Prohibition Amendment, in the Harrison Act against opiates, in the Marijuana Tax Act and in the Chinese Exclusion Act.

Such a metamorphosis of official policy is most readily enacted, and is subsequently most stable, when the proponents of deviant definition are well organized and highly motivated while the potential opponents are disorganized or indifferent. When that which is alleged to be dangerous is unfamiliar to those whose support in deviance definition is solicited, charges can safely be distorted; there is no reality against which to test them. Therefore, legislators unfamiliar with or indifferent to alleged deviance will feel safer in supporting than in opposing strong sanctions. Paranoid-like arguments are also grasped by moral entrepreneurs because of their commitments to their roles, and because they frequently must rationalize their own less morally justified interests in the deviance definition (for example, when the alleged deviants are their economic or social competitors, or when their status as law enforcers will be enhanced by extension of the laws they are hired to enforce). Numerous specific allegations of this sort can be cited: the Chinese Exclusion Act was passed by a Congress that was largely unfamiliar with Orientals and was swayed by a small group of California Caucasian politicians concerned mostly about their constituents' loss of jobs to Chinese (Schrieke, 1936: Chapter 1; VanderZanden, 1963: 117–118); the temperance movement, which brought about the Prohibition Amendment, is said to have expressed resentment by rural and small-town descendants of puritanical WASP immigrants against social status threats from less puritanical new migrants (Timberlake, 1966; Gusfield, 1966; Sinclair, 1962); the Marijuana Tax Act and Uniform Narcotics Control Acts are reported to have been enacted largely because distorted accounts of the effects of these drugs were circulated by a not disinterested leadership of the Federal Bureau of Narcotics (Lindesmith, 1968: Part II; Becker, 1963: 135–146).

While in the history of deviance definition, government policy often changes suddenly from permissiveness to prohibition or exclusion, subsequent change is likely to be less abrupt. Instead of switching back to permissiveness, there usually comes first—or permanently—the introduction of regulation and licensing. This applies particularly to deviant consumption and selling, and it reflects the difficulties of law enforcement. Because the people involved in these crimes do not regard themselves as victims, they rarely inform the police of their transactions. Therefore, police can intervene in only a negligible percentage of such offenses. Prohibition changes to regulation when the devotees of an illegal type of consumption become sufficiently numerous to be an appreciable political bloc, and they gain support from others who object to the corruption of law enforcement and to the subsidy of criminal enterprise that is a consequence of the popularity of illegal consumption.

The sequence of permissiveness to prohibition to regulation was most dramatically illustrated when, in 1918, the Prohibition Amendment was passed by ten more states than necessary for adoption, but largely because of its unenforceability it was repealed fourteen years later almost as quickly as it was adopted. It was replaced by laws regulating the character of purveyors, the hours and places of sale, and the age and condition of purchasers of alcoholic beverages. Less dramatically, we switched years ago in most states from nonregulation to prohibition of public gambling, but we now are increasingly permitting its reestablishment as licensed or government-owned enterprise. Regulation of opiate use also is now occurring through licensing the distribution of methadone to addicts. This is a synthetic opiate which can be taken orally in cheap and long-lasting doses; it has been many times as effective as any other method for which data on cross-sections of the addict population are available—if effectiveness is measured not by the elimination of drug dependence but by ending the crime and the neglect of personal health and of family that are associated with heroin use in our society (Dole, *et al.,* 1968, 1969; Gearing, 1970; Jaffe, 1970; Jaffe, *et al.,* 1970).

The difference between generations in familiarity with various types of drug use, demonstrated in Table 3, suggests that these forms of deviance will become expressions of normative conformity in a few decades, when the present youth grow older. This clearly is what happened with the use of alcoholic beverages in the decades following 1930. However, such a pattern is far from certain for all drug use. Waves of acceptance followed by general rejection have occurred in the use of several substances in a number of countries, notably the ether craze in Britain, the absinthe fad in France, and the postwar methedrine boom in Japan (Brill and Hirose, 1969). Some clues as to possible trends in the United States are suggested by the survey finding that those who reported knowing users of marijuana and amphetamines (doubtless including many who themselves were users) were more favorable in their descriptions of the effects of these drugs than those who said they did not know users, but those who said they knew users of LSD or heroin described the effects of these drugs more unfavorably than did those who did not know users (Glaser and Snow, 1969: Part 3). Observers of the drug use world report that the LSD craze in the 1960s reached a peak and then declined somewhat before the decade terminated. It may well be that marijuana and possibly amphetamine use will ultimately be regulated and accepted, while LSD or heroin use, glue-sniffing, and perhaps nonmedical use of barbiturates will continue to be regarded as deviant, because there are likely to be sufficiently persistent negative reports on their effects to prevent their ever achieving an extremely high popularity.

Kai T. Erikson (1966) traced the change in targets of deviance definition by seventeenth century Massachusetts Puritans from the Antinomian "heresy" to Quakerism and to witchcraft, in arguing that a society keeps fairly constant the extent of conduct that it treats as deviant. This constancy is ascribed to two factors in society: (1) its need to define something as deviant in order to identify the boundaries of its behavior norms, and (2) the limited capacity of its social control machinery. A striking feature of Erikson's data on the seventeenth century, however, is the fact that a much greater range of behavior was regarded as seriously deviant then than now. America's Puritan background includes legal sanctions against "persons who drank too much, who were 'without the use of their reason'; who lived a scandalous life, who dressed in inappropriate clothes or let their hair grow too long, who swore, bragged, or talked too much, who disobeyed their parents or engaged in frivolous games" (Erikson, 1966: 168). There were also court orders against people who spent their time "idly and unprofitably," who were "common coasters, unprofitable fowlers, and tobacco takers," who were accused of cursing (even when only cursing livestock), who were single and lived alone instead of with "an orderly family," and who wore "a silk hood" (Erikson, 1966: 169).

The Puritans left England because they sought to establish a colony "of saints," of people with much more ascetic behavior norms than prevailed elsewhere. While the other colonies were more tolerant of deviance, the Puritan influence may well account for the greater regulation of what is socially acceptable that has often distinguished the United States from Europe and from other countries founded by Europeans. At the same time, it is clear that deviance definition has been far from constant. In the United States and in other countries it seems clearly to diminish in range of behavior or status with which it is concerned whenever there is a declining influence of religious or political orthodoxy, or a growth of urbanism, secular education, autonomous mass media, or other sources of intercultural contact and communication.

In view of the foregoing, questions such as whether the proportion of the total population or of all behavior that is labelled deviant has declined, remained constant, or increased are absolutely moot. We cannot know whether, when some types of deviance decrease, there are compensatory increases in other types. We know that behaviors classified as deviant because they are predatory increase cumulatively as societies and cultures become more complex, while many types of performance, consumption, and belief cease to be labelled deviant; nevertheless we cannot measure one against the other. This is the case because we have no meaningful common units for measuring, adding, and comparing different types of deviance—for example, alcoholism, robbery, manic depression, rape, and belief in witches—to assess trends in total deviance.

Emile Durkheim is cited in support of the deviance constancy argument because he pointed to the function of deviance definition in maintaining societal authority, and because he predicted therefore, that crime will always exist—even in "a society of saints"

(Durkheim, 1950: 68–69). It should be noted, however, that he also predicted growth in the range of behavior that is tolerated as societies shift from mechanical solidarity, based on homogeneity in cultural background and norms, to organic solidarity, based only on common broad values necessary to make the division of labor viable—values such as honesty and responsibility (Durkheim, 1947; Parsons, 1968). The mass media, especially television, accelerate acceptance of deviant performance, consumption, and belief by searching out the unusual as newsworthy and portraying it until it becomes familiar.

While the long-run trend seems to be the designation of fewer types of behavior or statuses as deviant, there are also short-run fluctuations in deviance definition, as well as locational variations within societies. In the "safety valve" holidays of New Year's Eve and Mardi Gras, and in many other party occasions, the usual definitions of deviance are relaxed. Barrooms of various types institutionalize distinctive normative standards on a daily basis, facilitating the segmentation of life, with different criteria of conformity in various locations (Cavan, 1966). Indeed, the change in behavior we call "drunkenness" is explained as a product of new social expectations when a person is defined by himself and others as "drunk," as much or more than as a result of the physiological effects of alcohol (MacAndrew and Edgerton, 1969).

There are also short-run or local increases in the number of persons defined as deviant. Many people suffer rejection through being defined as deviant by association; the spouses, children, siblings, and parents of a murderer, suicide, mental hospital patient, or other person defined as deviant often share the stigma evoked by their relative. In addition, the scapegoating mechanism results in people who are slightly different from others, but socially accepted in times of general satisfaction, being readily blamed and discriminated against in times of social stress. This is illustrated by upswings in antiminority prejudice with unemployment. Finally, when a country is highly polarized on an issue, those outspokenly for the minority view may become unacceptable in most social circles. This has usually produced only a temporary increase in the number of persons regarded as deviant in the United States, as in the McCarthy era, and no clear-cut trends are evident. The definition of some people as deviant may fluctuate in frequency, but will probably never cease, for two reasons.

First, some types of behavior, primarily in-group predation, are inherently threatening to any social order, and will therefore always be regarded as deviant by most people. If world order grows, group boundaries will become less relevant to this definition and all predation will be regarded as deviant. Three factors make it unlikely that predation itself will cease: (1) it is a means of reducing personal tensions in coping with societal reward systems, (2) such reward systems are essential to social order, and (3) rewards are motivating only if they generate some tension. It is possible, of course, that there may be a decrease in violent forms of predation, since interpersonal violence is inversely correlated with education. Fraud or simply unfair or unsympathetic competition may be the major predations in a nonviolent society.

The second source of permanence in the phenomenon of people being rejected as deviant is simply social and cultural change. This applies particularly to nonpredatory types of deviance. We know that many predominant views and practices were once only accepted by a deviant minority. We should recognize, therefore, that many regarded as deviant today are the forerunners of the behavioral conformists of tomorrow. Finally, since change is continual and inevitable in society, we can also be sure that there will be new types of deviance in the future that we have not even dreamed of today.

REFERENCES

Becker, Howard S.
    1963   Outsiders. New York: Free Press.
Brill, Henry, and Tetsuya Hirose
    1969   "The rise and fall of a metamphetamine epidemic: Japan 1945–55," Seminars in Psychiatry 1 (May): 179–194.
Cavan, Sherri
    1966   Liquor License. Chicago: Aldine.

Dole, Vincent P., Marie E. Nyswander and Alan Warner
 1968 "Successful treatment of 750 criminal addicts," Journal of the American Medical Association 206 (December 16): 2709–2711.
Dole, Vincent P., J. Waymond Robinson, John Orraca, Edward Towns, Paul Searcy and Eric Caine
 1969 "Methadone treatment of randomly selected criminal addicts," New England Journal of Medicine 280 (June 19): 1372–1375.
Durkheim, Emile
 1947 The Division of Labor in Society. George Simpson, transl. New York: Free Press.
 1950 The Rules of Sociological Method. Sarah A. Solovay and John H. Mueller, transls. George E. G. Catlin, ed. New York: Free Press.
Erikson, Kai T.
 1966 Wayward Puritans. New York: Wiley.
Gearing, Frances
 1970 "Evaluation of methadone maintenance treatment program." International Journal of the Addictions 5 (September): 517–543.
Glaser, Daniel, and Mary Snow
 1969 Public Knowledge and Attitudes on Drug Abuse in New York State. Albany: New York Narcotic Addiction Control Commission.
Gusfield, Joseph R.
 1966 Symbolic Crusade. Urbana, Ill.: University of Illinois Press.
Jaffe, Jerome H.
 1970 "Further experience with methadone in the treatment of narcotics users." International Journal of the Addictions 5 (September): 375–389.
Jaffe, Jerome H., Charles R. Schuster, Beth B. Smith and Paul H. Blachley
 1970 "Comparison of acetylmethadol and methadone in the treatment of long-term heroin users." Journal of the American Medical Association 211 (March 16): 1834–1836.

Lindesmith, Alfred R.
  1968   Addiction and Opiates. Chicago: Aldine.
MacAndrew, Craig, and Robert B. Edgerton
  1969   Drunken Comportment. Chicago: Aldine.
Parsons, Talcott
  1968   "Durkheim." International Encyclopedia of the Social
          Sciences. New York: Macmillan, Free Press.
Quinney, Richard
  1970   The Social Reality of Crime. Boston: Little, Brown.
Schrieke, B.
  1936   Alien Americans. New York: Viking.
Schroeder, Herman G.
  1950   Auto Theft and the Dyer Act: A Case Study in the Soci-
          ology of Law. Unpublished master's thesis, Indiana Uni-
          versity.
Sinclair, Andrew
  1962   Prohibition. Boston: Little, Brown.
Timberlake, James H.
  1966   Prohibition and the Progressive Movement: 1900–1920.
          Cambridge, Mass.: Harvard University Press.
VanderZanden, James W.
  1963   American Minority Relations. New York: Ronald.

AUTHOR INDEX

SUBJECT INDEX